SECONDS TO LIVE OR DIE

To Megan:

May you and your
family never need
any of this.

All the best,

Rob Montgomery

SECONDS TO LIVE OR DIE

LIFE-SAVING LESSONS FROM
A FORMER CIA OFFICER

ROBERT
MONTGOMERY

GARDE BIEN

SECONDS TO LIVE OR DIE
Life-Saving Lessons from a Former CIA Officer

ISBN   978-1-5445-0949-5 *Hardcover*
       978-1-5445-0948-8 *Paperback*
       978-1-5445-0947-1 *Ebook*

This book is dedicated to my wife, my family, and the operations officers and paramilitary professionals of the Central Intelligence Agency.

CONTENTS

DISCLAIMER

All statements of fact, opinion, or analysis expressed are those of the author and do not reflect the official positions or views of the Central Intelligence Agency (CIA) or any other U.S. Government agency. Nothing in the contents should be construed as asserting or implying U.S. Government authentication of information or CIA endorsement of the author's views. This material has been reviewed by the CIA to prevent the disclosure of classified information.

Anyone practicing the techniques in this book does so at his or her own risk. The author and the publisher assume no responsibility for the use or misuse of information contained in this book or for any injuries that may occur as a result of practicing the techniques contained herein. The illustrations and text are for informational purposes only. It is imperative to practice the techniques shown under the strict supervision of a qualified instructor. Additionally, one should consult a physician before embarking on any demanding physical activity.

INTRODUCTION

MARINES, ESPIONAGE, PREDATORS, AND SHEEP

In any moment of decision, the best thing you can do is the right thing, the next best thing is the wrong thing, and the worst thing you can do is nothing.

—THEODORE ROOSEVELT

It's the fall of 2019, and I find myself in the Middle East working for a defense contractor on the heels of a thirty-seven-year career in government: three as a United States marine and thirty-four as an operations officer in the Central Intelligence Agency. As I write, my youngest daughter has turned four, my oldest son is an infantry officer in Afghanistan, my other son is in Air Force tech school, my oldest daughter is teaching in Greece, and I have two other boys under the age of ten. Like fathers the world over, I want to believe they are growing up in a safe world. But how safe is it?

A sampling of events from the past eighteen months reveals a wide range of violent encounters. Sri Lanka experienced a massive terrorist attack that killed in excess of 250 innocent people attending church and brunch at upscale hotels. Hundreds were injured. One hundred and fifty miles outside of Riyadh, in a town called Zulfi, four militants were killed, and three security force members were injured in an attack. (Curiously, there has been little Western press coverage of the latter.) Iran attacked Saudi oil production facilities, almost sparking a regional war. A man with a rifle in New Zealand slaughtered fifty-one people in a mosque and injured over thirty more. In a synagogue in Southern California, a sixty-year-old woman was killed and several people injured. At a Walmart in Texas, twenty people were murdered and twenty-seven more injured. Even a garlic festival in California became a scene of mass murder. Every news hour reveals yet another murder of a woman at the hands of a man, usually someone known to her. We live in dangerous times.

Train stations, buses, resorts, tourist venues, entertainment spots, and airports have all been targeted by terrorists in the past several years, and crime is something that weighs on us all—no matter the locale. Chances are you know someone who has been the victim of a serious crime or incident, or you have been the victim yourself.

CIA operations officers are trained to be situationally aware. It's imbued in our DNA from our earliest days in training and throughout our careers. Being situationally aware allows us to safely navigate the streets of cities and conflict zones all over the world, usually at night and in some of the most dangerous places on the planet. Working in the shadows, sifting out potential threats from the norm, collecting intelligence, and protecting human sources who put everything on the line to provide the U.S. Government with information. Situational awareness is knowing when something is wrong. The sense that alerts you when something doesn't feel right, that some-one is watching you, or that something is about to happen. The activation of your "sixth sense" in enough time to affect an outcome. It's a skill that can be honed. More than just a buzzword, it's what keeps you safe—until it doesn't.

Plans go wrong. No one can predict when violence will be visited upon them, and it can happen in the most innocuous places and when you least expect it. In 2002, tourists in the beautiful Indonesian island of Bali experienced two bomb-ings by Jemaah Islamiyah operatives: one at Paddy's Pub and another at the Sari Club, which resulted in 202 deaths and hundreds injured. That was the night suicide bombing made its debut in Indonesia. In January 2019, members of Al-Shabab attacked the luxury Dusit Hotel in Nairobi, Kenya, and killed over fifteen persons. In September of 2017, a teenager planted an improvised explosive device (IED) and packed it full of knives and shrapnel on a London train. The device misfired but still injured thirty people. In July 2016, a nineteen-ton cargo truck was used to drive into crowds of people celebrat-ing Bastille Day on the Promenade de Anglais in Nice, France, killing 86 people and injuring 450 others. The list of individual criminal assaults and terror attacks seems endless. An ever-growing spiral that shakes society to the core.

The sheer number and audacity of terrorist incidents and crime statistics the world over can feel so overwhelming that it is easy and natural to try to simply not think about it—to shut out of our minds the possibility that we could become the victim of a violent crime or a terrorist event. We rationalize the exclusion of such a possibility with thoughts like, "That only happens to other people," "I would never put myself in that kind of situation," "The chances of that happening to me are remote," "The authorities will handle it," or the more philosophical "It's in God's hands." With such an outlook, you are simply playing the lottery, only you are betting your life.

In the book *On Combat* by Dave Grossman and Loren Christensen, they describe a discussion with a retired colonel and Vietnam War veteran who explains that people generally fall into three categories: sheep, wolves, and sheepdogs:

> "Most of the people in our society are sheep. They are kind, gentle, productive creatures who can only hurt one another by accident." This is probably the category that most people we know fall into. They are the predominant members of society. They hold the values of our country and are our friends and neighbors. Then there are the wolves, and the wolves feed on the sheep without mercy.

The wolves are the sociopaths among us. People like Ted Bundy, Ted Kaczynski, and John Wayne Gacy are among the most well-known sociopaths in modern times and only because they were caught. But there is an untold number of sociopathic killers who have not been caught or achieved the notoriety of the aforementioned killers. These people will stab you at the ATM or target you for violence for their own amusement, desires, or beliefs. These types of predators have no empathy for those they victimize. None. Add to the mix that most child sexual abuse cases are committed by people known to the child.

"Then there are sheepdogs," the colonel went on, "and I'm a sheepdog. I live to protect the flock and confront the wolf." These people equate to our first responders and certain segments of our military, law enforcement, and intelligence services. Grossman sums up the veteran colonel's observation with the following:

> If you have no capacity for violence then you are a healthy productive citizen: a sheep. If you have a capacity for violence and no empathy for your fellow citizens, then you have defined an aggressive sociopath—a wolf. But what if you have a capacity for violence, and a deep love for your fellow citizens? Then you are a sheepdog, a warrior, someone who is walking the hero's path. Someone who can walk into the heart of darkness, into the universal human phobia, and walk out unscathed.

I love the concept of the sheepdog. That concept drove me into being a marine and later an operations officer with the CIA. But does that mean you have to become a first responder, a tier-one operator, or an operations officer in the CIA to possess sheepdog-like qualities? Not at all. What wolf wants to deal with a sheep who can think and fight like a wolf when necessary?

And so that is what this book is about. How to mentally and physically prepare yourself for the worst fifteen seconds of the worst day of your life. Those seconds could be when you are at home, at the ATM machine, at school, on a date, on a plane, at a five-star resort, at the office, at a place of worship, or simply driving home from work and witnessing or becoming part of a horrific car crash. Sometimes, there is no apparent rhyme or reason to violence. Other times, however, there is ample reason: you represent something someone hates enough to kill you for it, or you possess something a sociopath wants. Either way, you can prepare yourself in a manner that could mean the difference between life and death. The level of preparation can vary, and sometimes it's nothing more than a few seconds of forethought that can make a significant difference.

In intelligence operations and military operations, we plan for the worst and try to think of every imaginable contingency, and then we execute and hope for the best. Even then, plans rarely survive first contact, and often, a variation of the contingency plan saves the day. Experience matters, and learning from the experiences of others matters. What has become crystal clear to me after thirty-seven years of military and CIA service is that even a modicum of forethought can make the difference between success and failure and life and death.

Waiting for the moment violence is visited upon you to decide a course of action is less than ideal. At that point, it's too late to be pondering, "Why me?" or "What should I do?" That's the time to act. And how do you imagine you would fare if you had prepared for that moment? Or alternatively, if you were caught completely flat-footed with no prior experience or thought process to draw on?

Planning for the worst and looking at contingencies while understanding that things rarely go according to plan is really nothing more than a choice. Think of it as a lifestyle choice, like going to the gym every day. It's a commitment we make to ourselves and to those who depend on us: colleagues, subordinates, and our families. It's thinking about the unthinkable and incorporating those thoughts in a commonsense manner as we navigate our daily lives. This doesn't mean you have to live in a state of paranoia or get off of the grid and move to a bunker in Idaho. Rather, it's taking stock of your situation, honing your situational awareness, and listening to your instincts. It includes learning from the mistakes of others and taking active measures to avoid becoming a statistic. It's a decision to minimize the prospect of becoming a target of asocial violence or a terrorist act through common sense.

I've been extremely fortunate in my life to have had the training and mentoring of some highly extraordinary people, both in and out of government. I think the public would be extremely proud of what actually transpires on a daily basis within the true sheepdog cadres of our intelligence, military, and law enforcement communities. (I say "true" cadres, as membership alone is not a sufficient qualification, and all of these organizations have their fair share of pencil pushers, syntax monkeys, and risk-averse promotion-seeking bureaucrats.) The goal of this book, however, is to put some of the strategies and tactics I've learned over the years down into some easily digestible bites and to arm you with some practical knowledge and, more importantly, a mindset that will enable you to anticipate potential problems and ultimately to prevail in those fifteen seconds. I love sheep, and they represent all that is good in society. At the same time, in those crucial seconds, when the wolf is upon you, you must have a mindset that will enable you to meet the wolf as a wolf. As Theodore Roosevelt stated, "The worst thing you can do is nothing."

DREAM JOB—WORKING IN THE CENTRAL INTELLIGENCE AGENCY

I joined the Marine Corps in the late 1970s. The Vietnam War was over and the services and the public alike were getting over the social upheaval and trauma of those times. It was not a particularly good time to enlist. I can still remember the rage I felt when I was visiting a girlfriend at Mount Holyoke College in Massachusetts and was hitchhiking in uniform when a car full of teenagers drove by, and they delighted in honking the horn and giving me the finger simply because I was in uniform. Nonetheless, I enjoyed my time in the Corps, and when my enlistment expired, I decided to go to college. While in college, I was headed down the path of returning to the Marine Corps as an officer and had already completed half of the process. With my former enlisted time, I had excelled at the first half of the Platoon Leaders Course (PLC), one of the manners in which a college student can obtain a commission as an officer. The following year, I was studying in Japan for a year abroad when the Beirut bombing occurred on October 23, 1983. A Hezbollah operative drove a truck loaded with explosives into the Marine barracks and detonated it, killing 241. As events unfolded, it became clear that the chain of command failed those marines through restrictive rules of engagement and poor defensive measures. I started to have my doubts about my career path. Then a couple of months later, I was visiting the city of Hiroshima, one of two cities that experienced the atomic bomb in World War II. Standing at the memorial there was a powerful moment, and I was struck with how such an event should never occur again, particularly in the nuclear age when the stakes are so much higher. It was a galvanizing moment for me. I began thinking I could contribute beyond becoming a marine officer. I ultimately decided to resign from the PLC program. The following year, a CIA recruiter came to my campus, and I started the application process. After a barrage of tests and interviews interspersed with long periods of waiting and security clearance procedures, I was accepted. I was absolutely elated; it was a dream come true.

The CIA has had its fair share of criticism over the years—some deserved and some not—but one thing the agency does really well is training. And the operations training is among the best training in the U.S. government. Topics included tactical driving, firearms, explosives familiarization, undergoing interrogation and the psychological pressure that exerts, working with people who are helping the U.S. government collect intelligence, language training, first aid, and a myriad of other topics.

It was in that training and subsequent years abroad that I really started to hone my interest in protection and not just as it related to clandestine operations but how it related to all facets of life. While being a case officer is essentially a 24/7 job, what about our spouses and children who often accompany us to foreign posts and are vulnerable and at risk simply for being related to me and for their citizenship? There are many places abroad where simply being American is enough to hang a target on your back. And in a civilian paradigm, modern society is beset with violence and crime, and thus, sound protective measures are equally apropos.

As a father and husband, it is my profound hope that the content of these pages will be useful for my children and family—and perhaps to you and yours as well. With two beautiful daughters, I am keenly aware that the most victimized segment of society is women, and I want the women closest to me to be armed for the travails of life with the greatest possible chance of success. These pages contain some useful tips for mitigating the chance of becoming a victim. I hope you will benefit from them before the unthinkable happens because what is typical in human nature is that we often don't take precautionary measures until after an incident.

Robert Montgomery
Riyadh, Saudi Arabia

1

FEAR—KNOW IT. CONTROL IT.

If you had been at the Brussels Airport or the Shangri-La Hotel in Columbo, Sri Lanka, when suicide bombers detonated their vests—assuming you were not killed outright or injured—what might you have felt? Chances are, you have already felt something like it if you have ever happened upon a car accident that took place moments before or if you have ever come upon an act of violence such as a mugging or robbery. In the moments before the encounter, your parasympathetic nervous system, responsible for rest and digestion, was at work. Your heart rate was normal, and life was fine. At the moment of detonation/realization, your sympathetic nervous system (SNS) took over. This is commonly referred to as the "flight, freeze, or fight" reflex. Fear.

When the SNS is activated, evolution has trained us to instinctively hone our perceptions on the threat. In the blink of an eye, we experience the startle response and the first effects of fear. Adrenaline kicks in, and our heart rate rapidly increases. We start to sweat. Our bodies get a surge of cortisol that will enable blood to clot in the event of an injury. There is an increase in vascular activity in that our blood is redirected from our extremities to our heart. This is what can make fine motor skills—like loading a weapon's magazine or dialing 911—so difficult under severe stress. Our perceptions narrow, and our brain zeroes in on the perceived threat. Auditory exclusion (the ability to hear certain sounds) might occur, and our ability to think logically starts to degrade. Law enforcement officers in deadly encounters describe how they were so focused on the perp's handgun that they could see each bullet leave the barrel. A friend who was an air marshal told me once that when air marshals train with Simunitions (these are essentially high-end, high-velocity paintballs the size of a real bullet shot from a replica of an actual firearm—and they sting like hell) and are facing each other, there is a high rate of hitting the person's hands where they are holding the weapon. The reason is that the officers are so highly attuned to the threat of the other gun that it becomes their primary focus, and they unconsciously aim at the hands.

Immediately after the startle response, our heart rate changes drastically. A normal heart rate is 60–100 beats per minute (bpm). Dave Grossman described in his book *On Killing* how soldiers can operate at peak efficiency when their heart rates are about 115–145 bpm. After 145 bpm, most people will start to feel a deterioration in their complex motor skills. After about 175 bpm, most people's cognitive ability (their ability to think) starts to deteriorate, and they might start losing some peripheral vision and experience auditory exclusion. Once our bpm hits the 200s, our ability to think at all is vastly impaired. You can imagine that being near an explosion when you do not expect one could take your heart rate from a resting rate into the 200s in a proverbial heartbeat. Fear and animal instincts take root.

More simply put, when the shit hits the fan, our heart rates quickly increase—possibly to the point of not being able to think, move, or react. This equates to paralyzing fear, and the animal brain takes over. Blind panic ensues. Or another way to break it down: the incident happens, and our brains enter a stage of denial that could last a fraction of a second, hours, or anything in between. Then comes deliberation—what to do. Finally comes action—deliberate or otherwise. Blind panic can ensue at any point and in itself could constitute action. Denial is the most insidious response. Deliberation infected with denial is usually fatal.

So how do we control fear? The answer—as with most things in life—is easier said than done. But the concept is quite easy. If we understand what our body is experiencing in those initial moments—the accelerated heart rate and the onset of fear—then it is possible for us to enact a measure for regaining control. If we have considered what to do when the unexpected happens and know how to lower our heart rate, then when the incident occurs, we stand a chance of staving off blind panic and regaining control of the situation.

THE POWER WITHIN—LEARNING TO BREATHE

The explosion/incident occurs, and our body kicks in to automatic with the generation of chemical surges and heart rate acceleration. We react without thinking—the freeze, fight, or flight instinct. But then, in order to make a rational decision, we must first and foremost bring the heart rate down, and this is done in one simple manner: controlled breathing. Think about it. Just about every athletic endeavor from running to martial arts/boxing, yoga, meditation, and even childbirth is enhanced through controlled breathing. Breathing induces a relaxed state and in a moment of blind panic, bringing the heart rate down even a few beats can mean the difference between survival and death. So our first self-protective layer is understanding what is happening to our body when the incident occurs. The second protective layer is executing controlled breathing to bring the heart rate down.

In 2016, I observed a SEAL team jump in and close on a target compound in Afghanistan in an effort to locate a hostage. We could hear the team members talking to each other as they parachuted in, moved toward the objective, and then took out multiple threats as they closed in on the targeted compound. I was absolutely impressed with their manner of talking on the radio to each other. Every voice on the net was extraordinarily relaxed and every word spoken was done so clearly, calmly, and slowly. There are fewer endeavors more stressful than man engaged in the killing of man, and yet these professionals forced themselves to speak slowly and clearly—certainly not the fast pace of communications used by most soldiers engaged in a "troops in contact." But it makes eminent sense. It forces the participants to slow down and breathe, which reduces the speaker's heart rate and creates a sense of calm under extreme duress. Calmness under stress leads to better decision-making. From a leadership perspective, calm begets calm.

THE BREATHING CYCLE

The military and law enforcement communities understand the utility of "combat breathing" or "tactical breathing" when under stress. They know to focus on breathing by exhaling through the mouth for three to four seconds, pausing for three to four seconds, and inhaling through the nose for three to four seconds. In just a couple of cycles, you can start to bring your heart rate down into a more controllable zone. The same concept is employed by a sniper getting ready to squeeze off a round—he literally listens to his heart and synchronizes his breathing to it. Breath control is central in Zen meditation, yoga, and just about any sport you can think of. It is so pervasive in physical activity that one would be hard-pressed to think of an instance where holding your breath and tightening all your muscles would be conducive to any athletic endeavor. Even taking a fist to the stomach is easier to endure with an exhalation of breath and a loud *"kiah"* than simply holding your breath.

This breathing technique has helped me on numerous occasions over the years. One late afternoon, I was driving home from work in Northern Virginia. I was on a two-lane road when, suddenly, a station wagon driven by a mother coming from the opposite side of the road got too close to the curb on her side, and when she touched it, she overcorrected and came into ongoing traffic in my lane. She ran head-on into the car in front of me with each vehicle going about forty miles per hour. I was the first person to get to her car. As I approached the cars, I could feel my heart rate accelerating, and I anticipated with dread what I would see within the smashed and smoldering wreck. The front of the car was terribly mangled. She was not wearing a seat belt and was entangled in the wreckage to the extent that I did not see a way to move her. It was clear from her color and ragged breathing that she was slipping into death. If you have never seen death, there is an unmistakable feeling attached to it. You can just tell. Call it instinct or intuition, but in the few times I have witnessed it, I've never been wrong. Moreover, there is something particularly horrific about a car crash. It is unexpected and seemingly random, and it does terrible damage to human bodies.

I had to make a conscious effort to breathe. As I was doing so, I noticed there was a little boy about seven years old in the back seat of the car. He was frantic and wanted to get out of the wreckage. I was able to enter the car from the rear and pull him out. I carried him some meters away and placed him on the grass. From that moment, my focus was on the child, and within minutes, first responders arrived. The mother did indeed pass away at the scene, and the child suffered a broken leg. It was an example of unexpected, random violence that resulted in the death of a mother and a lifelong memory of horror for a child. When I reflected on the incident later, I concluded that breathing and talking to the child while doing a preliminary check for injuries helped rein in the feelings of fear and dread that I felt that day.

Some years later, I had a similar experience—only much closer to home both literally and figuratively. It's been said that one out of three car accidents happens within a mile from home. At that time, I was an instructor at one of our training facilities. My then twelve-year-old son was in a car pool headed home from school. They had just let out two other children at a different housing area on the facility. My son had removed his seat belt to let the other two children out, and when he got back in, he figured that he was on the facility and almost home—and didn't put on his seat belt. About ninety seconds later, as the car he was in rounded a curve, a painter working temporarily on the facility blasted through a stop sign and T-boned the car going around forty-five miles per hour. The car was pushed into the tree line. The driver was severely injured and rendered comatose for a couple of days, her daughter in the back seat suffered a ruptured spleen and broken ribs, and my son's head hit something in the car. He required brain surgery to survive the day. I was in the office, and my colleague, the husband of the driver, came in and said: "We've got to go. There's been an accident."

I remembered thinking, since we were on the facility, "How bad could it be?"

As we were driving to the scene of the accident, I told my friend, "Let's stop at the fire station on the way in case they've already been transported to the medical unit on the facility."

But the station was empty—a bad sign. We hastened up the road.

When we arrived at the scene, it was clear this was no fender bender. The scene was a hive of activity as a security officer had witnessed the accident and mobilized first responders within seconds of the crash. There were fire trucks and ambulances and dozens of people. As I ran up to the car my son had been in, I had that familiar feeling of dread. A trainee had also witnessed the accident. He was a former marine officer and had happened upon the accident within moments of it happening. He had extracted my son and was doing a preliminary check on his status while the fire crews and other ambulance crew were focused on my colleague's spouse, who was trapped inside of the wrecked vehicle. Of course, the person who caused the accident was fine.

My son was in a state of shock and not entirely responsive.

The trainee could see my visible concern and stated—not entirely convincingly—"He's OK."

I could see he was OK in the sense that he had his limbs and nothing seemed broken, but I could also see that he had hit his head.

Moments later, I was getting into the ambulance with him, and we were racing toward the hospital while my colleague's wife was getting evacuated by helicopter. As we were driving, I noticed that my son was becoming less and less responsive. Finally, he was not responsive at all and started to vomit. I knew just enough about trauma to understand that he had a serious head wound and that vomiting and the inability to stay awake were bad signs.

The emergency room was a flurry of activity as they cut away his clothing and conducted various tests. They quickly concluded that his brain was swelling and took him immediately into surgery. There is nothing like the feeling of walking beside your child on a gurney and getting close to the operating room only to have the nurse suddenly turn to you and state, "OK, this is where you say your goodbyes."

He survived the day and now has an impressive scar and plate in his head to remind him of the incident. Most parents recognize some version of this scenario. Kids get hurt, and it's a rare family that never has to go to the emergency room for some reason. But once again, deliberate breathing enabled me to maintain calm and understand the medical consequences of the moment, not only at the scene of the accident but to maintain calm and a clear mind while talking to the surgeon as well. Hysterical parents only exacerbate an already difficult situation.

While car accidents may be the most common form of unexpected violence most of us will encounter, there have been other occasions where controlled breathing helped me. In 2017, I found myself once again in Afghanistan at a facility I commanded far out in the provinces. We were heavily armed and were a formidable force, and other than harassing rocket attacks a couple of times a month, the enemy did not usually try to engage us directly, as it was always a losing proposition for them. There was the occasional minor ground assault and a couple of instances of suicide car bomb attacks over the years, but nothing major.

I usually exercised during lunch. That particular day, I was using a yoga app on my iPhone, and just as the nice lady closed out the session with "Namaste," a huge explosion rocked the compound. (I quipped afterward to my colleagues that for the rest of my life, I will clench when I hear "Namaste.") In any event, this explosion was way beyond the typical 105mm rocket. By this stage in my life, I had been in enough war zones and experienced enough stress to immediately recognize this was a serious incident. As I made my way to our spaces to get a status report, the rest of the contingent was mobilizing for a fight. I started the controlled breathing while jogging to our workspace to maintain a sense of calm. For this tour of duty, it was even more critical to present an aura of calm in the face of stress in order to demonstrate leadership to my officers. Calmness begets calm, whereas panic spreads.

We had an armed checkpoint, in essence a small fort, manned by an Afghan contingent about 300 meters from the perimeter. Over time the Taliban noticed that a small track had developed on its own, made by locals, and that the track passed by the gate of this particular checkpoint. As I was groaning through my final yoga stretch that day, a van loaded with about 2,000 pounds of high explosive made its way along that track, and as it came abreast of the entrance to the checkpoint, it made a hard left and punched through the gate. Maybe twenty seconds later, it detonated in the heart of the checkpoint, killing a dozen of the Afghan contingent.

Whenever such an event occurs, you should expect and be prepared for a follow-on attack. The initial moments after such an event have your mind racing as all hands go on full 360-degree alert: recon assets are launched, accountability takes place, initial reports (almost always wrong) start coming in, higher headquarters is alerted, medical staff rush to their places, and medivac helicopters are readied along with their escorts. Calmness begets calm, experience registers, and what were formerly drills (and we drilled often) get enacted for real. No follow-on attack took place that day. The perpetrators were identified and later dealt with. Just another day in that beautiful, war-torn country.

So in moments of stress, breathe. As Laurence Gonzales notes in his excellent book *Deep Survival: Who Lives, Who Dies, and Why*, "a panicked mind is a useless mind." Breathe. It will bring your heart rate down, and you will be better able to make an informed decision rather than letting the animal brain take over or, worse, causing a freeze while your body/mind contemplates whether to fight, freeze, or flee. Freezing rarely leads to the desired outcome, though—just observe any prey when they detect a predator. The ones who stay frozen wind up on the menu. Just ask a wolf.

KEY CONCEPTS

- Understand the physical effects of fear. Expect your heart rate to accelerate rapidly in conjunction with the startle response.

- Understand the relationship between your heart rate and the ability to think and use your fine motor skills. The higher your heart rate, the more difficult it is to use fine motor skills and to think.
- Know that you will go through a denial/deliberation/action cycle—then get to action as quickly as possible.
- Use breathing exercises to bring down the heart rate so that you can evaluate a situation and react accordingly rather than letting the animal brain take control.

2

ANY PREPARATION
IS BETTER
THAN NONE

DANGER FROM AFAR

We used to say that in the war zones, you would come back "a
hunk, a chunk, or a drunk," meaning that you would either (1)
exercise a lot, "hunk"; (2) eat a lot, "chunk"; or (3) drink a lot,
"drunk." I had opted for the first choice and made it a point to
exercise at lunch every day. One day as I emerged from the
shower, I noticed that my iPhone had a "motion detect" alert,
but let me back up.

Before I departed for Afghanistan, I put an Arlo security
camera by my garage door and one on the back deck. I didn't
really think they were necessary, but I thought it would be
a worthwhile precautionary measure for my wife, teenager,
and three young children. We live in a beautiful, crime-free
neighborhood in a small town. The idea of criminal violence
occurring in my neighborhood seemed a very remote possi-

bility. But the system was on sale, and I thought, "What the hell?" The two cameras came with an application that allowed me to view the scene on my phone or computer and would alert me when it had a "motion detect." Usually when there was a motion detect, it was due to a bug, a tree limb blowing in the wind, or one of the damn deer that enjoy eating my wife's plants so much. This time, however, when I casually looked, there was a Caucasian male wearing a ball cap, collar up, with a backpack, and he was using his phone to look inside my garage, and the time back home was 4:20 a.m. I suddenly had a sinking feeling, a growing rage, and a feeling of utter helplessness all at the same time. After watching for a few moments, I received a second motion detect on my back porch. That motion detection revealed an African American male dressed in a similar fashion, and he was testing the doors and windows. He had what looked like a possible firearm in his hand.

At this point, I made a FaceTime call to my wife. She was of course in a deep sleep. I told her as calmly as I could that I believed there were two intruders outside of the house and confirmed with her that our teenager was at home. He was. After she viewed the motion detects, I told her to go get the shotgun, load it, and tell me when she had it. She calmly stated "OK" and went to get it. I could hear her trying to load it, but she came back and said that she was having trouble. I told her to forget the shotgun, to go get the pistol and rack it one time (which would put a round in the chamber) and tell me when she was ready. She did this with ease because she had shot the handgun at least a half dozen times. After racking the slide, she was ready.

Now, a word about my lovely wife. She is, without exception, the nicest person I ever met. She will—literally—apologize to a fly before swatting it and then feel guilty about it afterward (noting that "it wanted to live too.") But now the prospect of intruders outside meant that our three youngest children—then aged two, five, and eight—as well as our seventeen-year-old, were now in danger, and her protective instincts were in full swing.

I told her to go down the hall, grab the teenager along the way, stand in the doorway of the kids' room, dial 911, speak slowly and clearly to the operator (she was born outside of the U.S. and has an accent), and most importantly, if anyone came up the stairs, to "shoot the shit out of them." Finally, I told her to call me back after she had done all that. She calmly signaled her understanding and took off down the hall. I was as amazed at her focus and determination as I was worried.

Meanwhile, as I was waiting for her to call me back, I received a third motion detect that revealed a third intruder also on the back deck, and I observed him testing the windows. By now, I was frantic and wondering why my wife had not called me back. I looked up the police department phone number on the internet and called them from my room in Afghanistan (the wonders of technology). They asked for my address, and when I told them, they stated that was the jurisdiction of the county police and put me on hold while they transferred my call. After what felt like a lifetime, the county police operator was on the line, and when I told her my address, she responded that they already had officers on the scene.

"Did you catch anybody?" I asked.

"No," she responded, "they fled the scene."

After what felt like an eternity, I was able to call my wife back. She told me that the 911 operator kept her on the line from the time she called, which was why she did not call me back. When the operator told her the patrol car had arrived, my wife still could not see it and correctly kept the operator on the line. Then when she finally did see the patrol car, she told the operator that she had a dog and a firearm and needed to put both away. She was amazing.

The police response was not impressive. They did not believe her initially until she showed them the video. We gave them copies of the videos, which they lost, and I had to resend them a few days later. They missed that one of the intruders had cut the screen of our porch door to access the porch. They claimed there were two intruders and not three until I pointed out in detail why there were three, to which they then agreed. Weeks later, they claimed that they had the suspects "under surveillance" (although having done my fair share of that throughout my career, I knew what kind of assets were required to truly put someone under surveillance, much less multiple suspects). And a few weeks after that, the police dropped the case because the prosecutor did not think the pictures were clear enough. The lesson there was clear: don't assume the authorities know what they are doing.

This is a hard lesson. We are taught from an early age that the authorities will respond appropriately. But the reality is responses by authorities will vary in effectiveness and professionalism. Don't bet your life or the lives of your family on the authorities being there the moment you need them. You must be your own first line of defense.

But the reason the police did not catch them was because the model citizen by the garage finally noticed the camera, told the others, grabbed the camera, and threw it in the bushes across the street as they beat a hasty retreat into a wooded area nearby. The police just missed them, although they found the car they had stolen down the street and eventually learned that they had gone down each house on our side of the street, testing doors and windows as they went. This knowledge was a relief to my wife, who was initially concerned that they knew she was alone with small children.

A MODICUM OF PREPARATION CAN MAKE ALL THE DIFFERENCE

The next day, as the gravity of the situation sunk in, my wife let her emotions about the event come out: a completely natural response to what had transpired and a necessary component to dealing with a traumatic event. But why had she performed so flawlessly in the moment and upon being woken up from a deep sleep, particularly given her gentle disposition and complete lack of exposure to this kind of stress? She never received any formal training. This intrigued me and also validated a decision I had made just before I left for my war-zone tour. In those frantic days before departure when the schedule is full of required training; updating wills; packing gear; ensuring automatic payment of bills; gathering passwords, important documents, and financial information for my wife; saying goodbye to my parents—not to mention spending time with my wife and the kids—I made a conscious decision to take a few minutes in the midst of the frenzy of tasks and ran a drill.

THE FAMILY DRILL

The drill was that someone was trying to enter the house at night. With my U.S. Army lieutenant son, we made my wife and other teenage son do a walk-through on their actions, and we talked about each step. "OK, you hold the handgun and stand here. Have our son stand there and control the kids. He can hold the other handgun if necessary. Keep a straight trigger finger until you have your sights on a target. Don't flag anyone in the room with your firearm. Don't wake the kids if you don't need to. Remember that if any shots are fired, it will sound extremely loud. Only shoot at an identified target." And so on. It only took about fifteen to twenty minutes to run through it a couple of times. None of us ever imagined we would ever need to enact the plan—our home was in a beautiful, crime-free, high-income area. And yet there were my wife and son doing exactly what we had practiced after being awakened from a deep sleep.

The lesson was clear. Have your family practice what they would do in various scenarios. These scenarios should include home intrusions and also what to do in the event of a natural disaster. Conduct several slow walk-throughs until you have a basic plan in place. Consider how to access any firearms or weapons, where to stand, and how to call for help. Discuss the physical aspects of fear with your family so they will recognize it when they feel it. Teach them how to bring down the heart rate through measured breathing. (You can use Grossman's moniker of "combat breathing" so the kids think it's cool). Impress upon them that controlled breathing will have an immediate, positive impact on their ability to think and act under any kind of stress. Work through any issues that might crop up. Is there a medical kit in the house? Is it accessible, and is everyone versed in the basics of stopping a bleed? Can the kit handle one or more gunshot wounds? This is the time to work it out and imprint your anticipated actions into your body of experiences. This kind of rehearsal for what could possibly be the worst moments of your or your family's lives is well worth the investment for the relatively small amount of time that it takes.

Figures 1–3. When I was deployed to a war zone, these three pillars of society tested my doors and windows while my wife and children slept inside (photos are still shots from my Arlo video camera). They would have met a unique reception between my armed wife and son and our German shepherd had they actually entered the house. I fantasized for months afterward that they would come back when I was home. Was the middle pillar armed?

THE POWER OF SLOW PRACTICE AND VISUALIZATION

Slow practice. In firearms training, there is a saying: "Slow is smooth and smooth is fast." This is a simple yet extremely important training concept that is applicable to all facets of self-protection from hand-to-hand combatives to shooting to executing a family drill. Practice slowly. If you can execute a family drill correctly several times with an easy pace and in control, then when speed is applied, your execution will be about the same. In hand-to-hand fighting, slow practice is absolutely essential to put your strikes on target. (Poking an eye gets you everything, whereas missing by an inch and poking the forehead gets you nothing.) Yet the vast majority of martial arts training overlooks this simple concept and encourages speed from the onset of training—and thus breeds sloppy targeting. Slow repetition applies muscle memory so that the more you imprint a drill, the less you will have to think about it in actual execution. Working through any protective measure slowly will make the execution smooth and ultimately enhance speed naturally. Visualization in self-protection is taking each contingency and visualizing the outcome.

Many professional athletes use slow practice and visualization to enhance their physical and mental games. Watch a pro golfer as they start to set up. Prior to stepping up and hitting the ball, they visualize every aspect of their shot from striking the ball to its flight to where it will land to how the ball will roll. And if you don't play golf, don't start—the golf gods are not benevolent gods!

When martial artists break objects, they don't usually just walk up and hit them; rather, they carefully and slowly trace their strike a couple of times to visualize where and how they will hit the target, and then they execute the strike.

Pilots use slow practice in "chair flying" or procedure trainers, where they can learn, practice, and imprint sequences of actions in the event of an emergency situation in a relaxed environment. (Who would you rather have pilot your plane, the pilot who blew this training off or the pilot who incorporated such training on a regular basis?)

Two of the most effective hand-to-hand combat styles—Injury Dynamics, based in San Diego, California, and Target Focus Training in Las Vegas, Nevada—incorporate slow practice extensively. Master Instructor Chris Ranck-Buhr of Injury Dynamics advocates this methodology to imprint correct targeting and structure in striking. In Chris's words, "The brain can only go where the brain has been before." This means that in a moment of crisis, there will be fear, and for most, it will degrade a person's ability to think through to a solution. With the speed of a supercomputer, our brains review prior experiences in order to achieve a solution and allow it to cope with the issue at hand—deliberation. Slow, repetitive practice in a variety of scenarios imprints potential solutions. This method of practice will ingrain solutions to problems and, in a crisis, allow your brain to run through its index of experiences to arrive at a course of action. Slow practice also enables perfection in targeting, and as Chris likes to say, "It's better to work out the problems and get it right 200 times in the school than to bet your life figuring it out on the street the first time it happens." Their incorporation of slow practice makes them unique in the world of combatives training. An added benefit to this methodology is that people of advanced age, small stature, or with physical limitations can practice fighting skills effectively and efficiently.

The book *The Talent Code* is a fascinating exploration about "deep practice" (slow practice) and imprinting correct form/techniques for all manner of endeavors. Author Daniel Coyle describes his visit to a Russian tennis school with one indoor court, no private lessons, and a producer of top-twenty women players. Coyle discovered that the school incorporated slow-motion practice extensively, and the success of its graduates is undeniable.

In basic firearms training at the CIA, we apply the same concept. Learning to draw the weapon from the holster; bringing the hands to chest level; pushing them out while acquiring the target, feeling the trigger pull, and squeezing off the round. We dry fire (no ammunition) in this manner slowly and repeatedly. After imprinting the mechanics of the draw, we then fire with live rounds. Speed is gradually introduced as muscle memory is imprinted. By the end of the training evolution, officers who have never shot in their lives can place two well-aimed rounds into the target within two seconds.

So for drills, keep it slow and keep it precise. Slow practice will imprint the desired outcome in the repository of experiences in our minds so that when under stress, we will have already worked out a solution. Slow is smooth and smooth is fast, and the concept applies to all facets of protection, from walking through your house in a home-defense scenario to firearms training to hand-to-hand combatives and to competitive sports.

KEY CONCEPTS

- Drill with your family for contingencies with the understanding that the actual event will not necessarily be as you drilled but likely some variation of it.
- Apply the concept of slow practice when executing your family drill. Slow practice ensures understanding and muscle memory and imprints doing an action correctly. The converse, going at speed with imperfect execution, reinforces mistakes. This is applicable to just about any aspect of self-protection.
- Any preparation is better than none. Sometimes, even a few seconds of forethought can mean the difference between life and death.

3

DISCERNING THE EVIL AMONG US

We all have images in our minds about what evil people look like. In the terrorism realm, it's the faces of people like Osama bin Laden, Khalid Sheikh Mohammed, Hambali, ISIS fighters, and fighters for the Taliban and Haqqani network. But the first time you walk down the street in Islamabad, Karachi, Kabul, or anywhere else in that part of the world, the newcomer discovers that *everyone* looks like those people. Everyone has a similar style of dress, headwear, and facial hair, and it quickly becomes apparent that the only way to distinguish friend from foe is when they are trying to kill you or you possess corroborated intelligence. A young nineteen-year-old combat arms soldier or marine usually figures this out within hours or days of arriving in the war zone. The good news is that the number of actual enemy combatants is far fewer than the general populace. The trick, then, is to figure out who is who.

In a civilian paradigm, it's just about the same in terms of the threats among us. The difficulty centers in our near complete inability to distinguish predator from decent citizen. It would be convenient if predators walked around with swastikas tattooed on their foreheads like Charles Manson. They don't. Most predators—at least on the surface—blend into society, and they rely on surprise and overwhelming violence to get what they want. People like this can be roughly categorized, and understanding the traits of a predator may provide enough warning to obviate the element of surprise.

PREDATOR LABELS: SOCIOPATH, PSYCHOPATH, PSYCHOTIC—DO THEY MATTER?

A sociopath is basically a person who engages in antisocial behavior and lacks a conscience when doing so. They feel that rules and laws don't apply to them. Most likely, a sociopath grew up in an environment where antisocial behavior was the norm. Growing up among inner city gangs or a third-world child-soldier culture might encourage this type of personality development. But a sociopath still understands right from wrong.

A psychopath is a person who, like a sociopath, engages in violent or abnormal social behavior. Like a sociopath, he or she gets a thrill by taking advantage of people. There is a good possibility you know one. That's a sobering thought. Roughly 1 percent of the total population and 10 percent of the prison population fall into this category. Chances are you can think of one or more people who embody this description, whether it's an acquaintance, a childhood friend, family member, boss, or coworker. I have a relative who fits this description. He has repeatedly stolen from his parents and conned other relatives out of significant sums of money. All with a smile and all without an ounce of remorse or regret—a state of mind that is difficult for most of us to grasp. This is even more puzzling since he was raised in a loving and supportive family environment. Moreover, people in this category are often successful in their careers. They lie and manipulate to get what they want. And contrary to popular belief, they do understand right from wrong.

The sociopath and the psychopath share many traits. It is generally believed that a sociopath is molded by their environment, but a psychopath is born that way.

Now add to the mix the term "asocial." This type of criminal is synonymous with the sociopath and the psychopath. For our purposes, the terms are interchangeable—he is a predator. This is the person who robs you at gunpoint or attacks you at the ATM to get your money and shoots or stabs you anyway. Or attacks first and takes what he wants as his victim lies bleeding on the ground. You are simply a resource to them. This type of person is commonly found in criminal circles and in various terror organizations throughout the world.

A psychotic is someone who is mentally unstable to the extent of being out of touch with reality. They hear the voices and are usually much easier to identify. They are generally incapable of planning and executing a predatory strike against a victim and covering up the crime accordingly. They don't necessarily understand right from wrong.

A narcissist is also a master manipulator, lacks empathy, and is self-centered but does not have the violent traits of the sociopath or psychopath. We've probably all had bosses who fit that description (and probably wondered about some of the traits).

In the realm of self-protection, the distinctions are not important, other than to understand this: there are people among us who manipulate and take from other human beings without giving it a second thought. They are predators in the fullest sense of the word, and they have no empathy—they feel nothing for another human being. Decent, law-abiding people encounter extreme difficulty comprehending this mindset. We are both mesmerized and frightened by it. The sheep cannot fathom the mind of the wolf, but we are fascinated by the wolf as demonstrated by the central role of violent antagonists in our entertainment, whether out of Hollywood, in print, or computer gaming.

The predators among us are often difficult to discern. They blend into society relatively easily. This is precisely the trait that makes them so frightening. Let's look at some examples.

THE CHURCH LEADER

Dennis Rader was the BTK Strangler. (BTK was a moniker he gave himself that stood for "Bind, Torture, Kill.") He served an enlistment in the Air Force, had an associate's degree in electronics, and had a BA in administration/justice. He worked at the Wichita-based office of ADT Security Services from 1974 to 1988, where he installed security alarms as a part of his job. Later, he was a census field operations supervisor for the Wichita area in 1989. The last two jobs obviously took him door to door.

He was the president of the Christ Lutheran Church and a Cub Scout leader. In 1974, he tortured and finally killed the Otero family. The victims were father Joseph Otero, age thirty-eight; mother Julie Otero, age thirty-three; and two children, Joseph Otero Jr., age nine; and Josephine Otero, age eleven. Their bodies were discovered by the family's eldest child when he returned home from school. It is believed that between 1974 until his arrest in 2005, Rader killed and tortured at least ten people. Rader believed that the women he killed would be his sex slaves in the afterlife. And yet he blended into society so well that it took thirty-one years to catch him.

THE CLOWN

John Wayne Gacy was married twice and had two stepdaughters in his second marriage. On the surface, he led a normal life. In the 1970s, he became active in local Democratic party politics. In 1975, Gacy was appointed director of Chicago's annual Polish Constitution Day Parade. He supervised the annual event from 1975 until 1978 and, through that venue, was even photographed with then First Lady Rosalynn Carter in 1978.

He was a member of the local Moose Club and joined a clown club as "Pogo the Clown." Pogo performed at local parties, Democratic party functions, charitable events, and at children's hospitals. Between 1972 and 1978, Pogo the Clown murdered between twenty-five and thirty-three teenage boys.

THE MILITARY COMMANDER

Canadian Air Force Colonel David Williams was considered a model officer. His wife was an associate director of the Heart and Stroke Foundation of Canada. He was the officer in charge of Canada's largest air base and flew dignitaries such as Queen Elizabeth II, Prince Philip, and the Governor General and Prime Minister of Canada. He also killed two women and was charged with sexual assault (including that of a twelve-year-old girl) and eighty-two fetish-related break-ins. His computer contained thousands of pictures from his crimes and included multiple pictures of Williams dressed in underwear and bras he had stolen. He used these articles of clothing to masturbate while lying on the beds of his victims.

"DO NO HARM"—DOCTORS AND MEDICAL PERSONNEL

What about mild-mannered Donald Harvey, a hospital orderly who, between 1970 and 1987, murdered as many as eighty-seven mostly elderly persons in the hospitals he worked at?

Or British doctor Harold Shipman, who is possibly linked to as many as 236 patient deaths over a twenty-four-year period?

How about Frederic Pechier, a French anesthetist who was under investigation in 2019 for poisonings that lead to nine deaths? He is accused of tampering with anesthesia pouches to create an emergency in order to show off his talents. Police think he was possibly involved in sixty-six cases of cardiac arrests on patients—who were considered low risk—while undergoing operations. Victims were aged four to eighty.

Then there was German nurse Niels Högel, who admitted to administering fatal doses of medication to people in his care, killing at least one hundred patients between 1999 and 2005. In one instance, he was allowed to continue working for two days after being caught administering drugs to a patient that was not under his care. In those intervening two days, he killed yet another patient. Investigators believe he probably killed more, but many of his likely victims had been cremated.

THE HANDSOME SUICIDE HOTLINE VOLUNTEER

Ted Bundy's story made a resurgence in 2019. He killed at least thirty women in seven states between 1974 and 1978. In addition to being a serial killer, he was a kidnapper, rapist, burglar, and necrophiliac (someone who engages in sexual intercourse with a corpse). He was regarded as handsome and charismatic, traits that he exploited to win the trust of his victims. He would typically approach them in public places, feigning injury or disability, or impersonating an authority figure before overpowering and assaulting them in secluded locations. He decapitated at least twelve victims and kept some of the heads as mementos in his apartment. On one instance, he broke into a sorority house and murdered his female victims in their sleep. In her excellent book *Dangerous Instincts*, retired FBI profiler Mary Ellen O'Toole recounts:

> If you were a young woman working late at the office, you might ask another employee to walk you to your car—just in case a dangerous stranger was lurking somewhere in the parking lot. The now famous crime writer Ann Rule did just that, years ago when she worked at a suicide hotline with a handsome young man whom she knew well and had befriended. He often walked her to her car at night and asked her to be careful. His name was Ted Bundy.*

THE RELIGIOUS MAN

Look at Gary Ridgway. A Navy veteran, he was convicted of murdering forty-nine women between 1982 and 1998, although it is believed the actual number of victims is much higher, as he confessed to seventy-one. Most of his victims

---

* Excerpt From: Mary Ellen O'Toole, PhD & Alisa Boman. "Dangerous Instincts." Apple Books. https://books.apple.com/us/book/dangerous-instincts/id440418155

were prostitutes or runaway women, and he would strangle them to death. Reportedly, while he was killing women, he concurrently went through a religious period in his life and was an ardent reader of the Bible. Sermons, at times, literally brought him to tears. His so-called religious zeal was such that he went door-to-door proselytizing. To take his depredation to another level, however, he was a necrophile and often visited the corpses of his victims to have sex. Incomprehensible? Absolutely. The mind of a psychotic? Absolutely not. All of his murders were planned and executed accordingly, not to mention the careful disposal of the bodies and the acts of necrophilia. He loved the hunt and the feeling of power to dominate another person's life.

THE CARNIVAL WORKER

Carnival worker and drifter Tommy Lynn Sells is believed to be linked to at least twenty-two murders between 1980 and 1999. In one instance in 1999, he climbed through the window of the home of his target in Texas and into the room of a ten-year-old girl, where he proceeded to sexually assault her and then killed her with a knife. As he was about to leave, he noticed that his victim's thirteen-year-old friend was in the top bunk, paralyzed with fear after hearing the death of her friend. Sells returned to the bunk bed and calmly told the girl to put her hands down, at which point he sliced her throat and left. Miraculously, this girl had the wherewithal to walk a quarter of a mile to get help. Her description of events allowed police to locate and arrest Sells.

THE FORMER COP

Joseph DeAngelo was a father of three daughters, a Navy veteran, and a police officer from 1973 to 1979. He is believed to have killed at least thirteen people and committed over fifty rapes and over one hundred burglaries. He thrived on the fear of his victims. He would break into a home, tie up the husband, and place him on his stomach on the floor. He would then go to the kitchen and retrieve some plates, which he would place onto the back of the husband, and he would warn him that he was taking the wife into the next room, and if he heard the sound of plates, he would kill the wife and come in and kill him. He enjoyed killing his victims with a hammer. And if that weren't enough, he would often taunt his rape victims later with phone calls. He was finally arrested based on DNA genealogy investigative techniques in 2017. The ultimate manipulator, when authorities arrested him, he was cutting his grass. When he showed up in court, he was in a wheelchair.

THE VAGABOND

As of late 2019, Samuel Little may be America's most prolific killer, as the FBI believes he may have killed up to ninety-three women across the country. He remembered each victim to the extent that he could sketch out each of their faces.

And the list goes on and on—and these are only some of the more notorious killers who have been caught.

What about the ones who are still among us? Or the different shades of sociopaths—criminals like the "petty" criminal who will visit violence upon a victim with little or no provocation? Or a kid who will come from behind and engage you in the "knockout game"—striking a victim from behind to attempt a single hit knockout. What about the home invader who will beat an elderly woman senseless for no particular reason? Or the rapist who likes to watch the girls jog by at the city park?

PARANOID YET?

People who are mentally ill and genuinely psychotic are not usually a problem. They tend to be the easy ones to identify—the mumbling street person on the way to work. On the other hand, sociopaths and psychopaths constitute the real predators among us. These predators share certain qualities:

- They love the hunt.
- They have no empathy for another human being. None.
- They exalt in the power of holding a human being's life in their hands.
- They are often highly skilled at manipulation.

Former police officer, doctor, political activist, military officer—at first blush, predators may seem normal. But they do exhibit subtle signs of their proclivities and certainly to those who know them. As a stranger, they may start to engage you with a question or a comment. You may feel a passive-aggressive manipulation attempt, perhaps insisting on helping you with your groceries or some other task—that is when many victims start to "cross-examine" themselves—in essence overriding their instincts through denial and deliberation. Retired Former FBI profiler Mary Ellen O'Toole points out that we can be blind to risk because:

- We rely too heavily on first impressions. (At first, this might seem to be at odds with listening to your instincts, but that is not necessarily so. If something makes you uneasy, react accordingly. If a person makes you feel comfortable, don't automatically assume all is well. Simply remain internally vigilant, especially in cases where you or members of your family could be placed in a compromising position).

- We implicitly trust a recommendation from a trusted source. (Think of your friend who recommended a contractor to work on a project in your home.)
- We tend to believe superficial details of normalcy. (Ted Bundy was handsome, John Wayne Gacy was active in politics and joined a clown club that benefitted charities, Colonel David Williams commanded a base and was considered a model officer, and Dennis Rader was active in church and a Cub Scout leader.)
- Our own personalities cloud our judgement: "It will be fine. I don't want to be rude."
- Our past experiences cloud our judgment: "I've never had a problem before. It's probably nothing."
- We are susceptible to simply denying something bad might be happening when under stress.

THE WOLF WE KNOW

We are taught from childhood to be wary of strangers and rightly so. But no one warns us about exercising awareness with people familiar to us. Murders are four times more likely to be committed by persons known to us than by strangers. The National Center for Victims of Crime states that 60 percent of children are sexually abused by someone in their social circle, and offenders are overwhelmingly male. Think about that. The chances are heavily weighted in favor that you or a family member will be victimized—not by a stranger—but by someone you already know.

All of the aforementioned predators were "normal" on the

surface. In many cases, the killers had overly domineering mothers and usually suffered under difficult family circumstances growing up. Mommy issues are way beyond the scope of this book, but when these killers were brought to justice, no doubt neighbors and acquaintances expressed shock, as "he was a nice guy" or "he always said hello." But the fact of the matter is, in hindsight, the signs were there. The dots only needed to be connected.

All of them had telltale signs of the evil within. In his book *The Killer Across the Table*, retired FBI profiler John Douglas identifies three general behaviors common among many killers in their adolescence:

- Bed-wetting
- Starting fires or an obsession with fire
- Cruelty to animals

Now, this does not mean that every child who has bed-wetting issues or a kid who doesn't care for dogs or cats is going to become a serial killer. I am also not talking about a kid who takes an interest in hunting. But if friends or family start noticing a combination of the identified behaviors, such as an obsession with fire and taking pleasure in the pain of an animal, it should set alarm bells ringing, for as they say, the best predictor of future behavior is past behavior.

KEY CONCEPTS

- Predators exist. They live among us and often blend into the fabric of society. For the sane and rational person, it is difficult to imagine that such cruelty and lack of empathy is possible from a fellow human being. They exist, and we must accept it.

- Predators are masters at manipulation. Women and children, in particular, are vulnerable, as there is often predilection to not want to be rude or offend. The predator knows this and uses it to his advantage.
- Strangers are indeed dangerous. But we are far more likely to be victimized by someone known to us.

4

PREDATORY TACTICS AND VIOLENCE AGAINST WOMEN

As a sane member of society, how is it possible to understand a predatory mindset? To wrap our minds around this issue, we have to first acknowledge that there are people among us who have no empathy for another human being. They define evil in the fullest sense of the word. This is actually a difficult concept for many to accept. I know people close to me who are kind and trusting. They make the world beautiful. Most of them will go through life extending help to others and being active in church and the community. They embody all that is right in society. They care. They—most of all—have a difficult time understanding the predator's mindset. It is simply too repressive of a thought process to admit to; it is akin to the innocence of a child. If the gods are smiling upon these wonderful people, most will go through life with an unwavering belief in the goodness of humans and never have to confront this brutal reality. But I would contend that they are counting on the odds and betting their lives in the process.

VIOLENCE AGAINST OUR WIVES, MOTHERS, DAUGHTERS, AND SISTERS

Ask any woman what she did this week to avoid unwanted sexual attention or an assault. The answers will be varied but, rest assured, there will be some kind of answer to illustrate precautions taken. Then ask a man, and you will likely be met with a blank stare. Unfortunately, examples of women being victimized in our times are endless. And in that, we really arrive at a crucial waypoint in the issue of self-protection. How can a woman identify behavior that suggests she is a target? And if so, what concrete steps can she take to effectively take control of the situation?

Almost every survivor of an assault will later indicate that there was "something wrong" that they could not clearly identify at the moment. A feeling or sixth sense that gave them pause—if even just momentarily. One young teaching assistant related her experience:

> I left one of the university buildings at 10 p.m., as I held an extra help session until that time. Although it was dark, students were around campus, just as at many universities. The libraries were open late. A nearby convenience store had just closed for the evening. There was not a lot of traffic on the road, but some cars passed by.

> I saw him at a corner of the street when I came out of the university building and passed him. He might have nodded or said hello. I remember thinking that he looked unfamiliar. Although there were a few thousand students on campus, after a few years, you recognize most faces. He didn't look like a student—he was a bit older and did not have a backpack. He

didn't look creepy or lecherous, but he did look out of place. He started walking behind me.

As I turned down my street, I had a reason to stop at the first house, so I turned onto the path and walked to the door. I chatted briefly with my friend at the door. He continued walking down the street. Then I left to walk home. I did not see him. It was three blocks—less than a tenth of a mile—of single-family houses and a few duplexes, mainly rented by students (with a few families mixed in). There were streetlights, but there were a few spots that were not well lit.

After about a block of walking, I heard footsteps behind me. These stood out in my mind because they made a tapping sound. Most students at this time wore sneakers; this person was wearing shoes with hard heels. I thought it might be the man I had seen at the corner and felt uneasy, but I didn't turn around to look. It sounded like he was walking quickly. I noticed that the convenience store was dark. I was about six houses from home. Some houses had lights on; some were dark.

There was a narrow strip of grass between the sidewalk and the road; in a few places there were trees in this strip.

I could hear him walking faster, and he caught up to me from behind, at which point he made an innocuous comment about the weather, and I recognized him as the man from the corner.

He asked, "Do you live around here?"

I wasn't going to tell him where I lived, so I said something vague about just up the street.

He asked if I lived by the fire station (which was beyond my house), and I said no.

I knew something was wrong. But I didn't want to be rude, and I didn't think anything could happen to me. I kept thinking, "Keep walking and talking. You're almost home." I had been at a religious retreat the weekend before, and I fixed on that. I started to tell him that I had been in Vermont (at this retreat), and the sky was so clear and so many stars were visible that you can't usually see.

We came to a slight dip in the road, where there was a big shady tree along that strip of grass that always felt a bit dark to me. I could see my own house on the corner.

He grabbed my right arm above the elbow, placed something sharp against my neck, and said in low voice, "Don't scream or you're dead."

We had just come to a driveway. He pulled me along that driveway and into the backyard of a darkened house. I could literally see my house and the room where my baby was sleeping. The yard dipped down a bit so that we would no longer be visible from the street.

He repeated, "Don't scream or you're dead," at least once.

I recall saying, "Why are you doing this?"

He pushed me onto the grass facedown and began striking me on the head with a blunt object. I put my right hand over my head and began screaming. He tried to cover my mouth with his hand, and I bit him. Just then, the owner of the house pulled into their driveway, and the headlights shined on us, and he ran away.

She reflected:

I have thought many times of things I could have done differently. I think the friend I stopped to see asked if I wanted her to call the campus escort service to drive me home, but it seemed too short a distance (it was a five-minute walk at the most), and the neighborhood felt safe. I could have asked her to call my husband and tell him to come to the front of the house to wait for me. I could have turned when I heard the footsteps and had a few moments to act. I could have screamed or shouted at the man to go away when he first came up to me. I could have tried to pause a step and maneuver behind him and begin walking in the street where the lighting was better. He took advantage of a dark spot where he needed only a couple of seconds to pull me out of view of anyone passing by. Getting even a few feet away would have made it more difficult for him to grab me... Recalling this reminds me how untrusting I was of my own feelings. I focused on some strange things—protecting my head, recalling our phone number, telling my husband to call our friend (that I had spoken to a few minutes before) to come stay with our daughter: these all have something to do with survival. But I also focused on other things that were not helpful—I didn't want to hurt his feelings by running away or yelling; I didn't want to bleed on a carpet (when I entered the couple's house to call the police). I don't know the right word for this other than a vague idea of doing what you are supposed to do.

Mainly, I knew something was wrong, but I just couldn't do anything about it, and I kept thinking that I would make it home OK.

She made it. She survived what was sure to be a deadly encounter. Her reflection on the events and her thoughts are profound and contain some powerful lessons about situational awareness, intuition, and courses of action. There is no doubt that if she were faced with a similar circumstance today, her mind would recall this experience, and she would take definitive action to mitigate the threat. A powerful lesson for all.

SURPRISE AND DOMINATION

To understand the mindset of a predator, we need to first break down the characteristics of a predatory strike. Every creature in the food chain exhibits some kind of preattack behavior. Sharks circle their prey before they attack. Dogs raise their hackles and growl. Elephants stamp and flap their ears, and snakes rattle or rear up prior to the strike. Humans, too, have preattack indicators, although they are not all the same, and some are more subtle than others. In the realm of social violence, these indicators are pretty obvious, and chances are you have seen them in the form of "the man dance" typical of adolescent males vying for territory and dominance ("What are *you* looking at?"). The danger in this this type of violence is that it can escalate into asocial violence quickly, like arguing over a parking space when one person pushes the other, and the offended party takes out a firearm and shoots his antagonist to death. Road rage incidents have this characteristic in spades. Or even if one person strikes the other, attempting to dominate and intimidate. But as the person who was hit falls, he strikes his head against the concrete, and what started out as social violence turns into homicide. But this social violence is easy to recognize (and for that matter, easy to avoid). All it requires is for one person to walk away—perhaps losing face within the man dance context but living to tell the tale.

Imagine how much society could benefit if the seventeen- to twenty-year-old male population understood this.

But real predators don't typically engage in social violence. They dominate with surprise and overwhelming brute force to get what they want. Most people never see them coming until the attack has been initiated.

Domestic abuse is also about domination. The abuse is (relatively) easy to recognize, albeit harder to avoid and walk away from. It usually starts as an overly manipulative and possessive relationship and escalates to verbal and physical abuse. But signs and levels of gradation are evident. Unfortunately, it is often the victim herself who can twist the facts to form a series of denials that ultimately keep her in the abusive relationship. But there is one thing that history has proven over and over again: if the woman believes her abuser can change, she is wrong. And the consequences for that misbelief are often deadly. If you are in a relationship with a person who wants to control you and is verbally or physically abusive, they will not change. That is an absolute. You must end the relationship—reach out for assistance—but at the end of the day, it has to be you who recognizes the problem, admits to the problem, and takes action to get out of a destructive relationship. I suppose if there is any positive outcome from this situation, it is the fact that, now more than any time in the past, there is recognition of the problem, and more resources are available than ever before to help women cope.

The predator seeks absolute domination. And to dominate, he must be close to you—within arm's length.

TRIGGERS TO PREPARE FOR THE FIGHT FOR YOUR LIFE

The unknown predator, on the other hand, is different and, often, more difficult to recognize. The asocial predator who attacks a stranger will exhibit some signs of his intentions, but these can be unnoticed by his victim. For example, women joggers attacked on the trail and women assaulted while returning to their cars in a parking lot. But even then, there are subtle—and not so subtle—signs one can look for that should trigger an alarm response:

- As you walk toward your car, a man comes up and asks you for the time, a light, or some other seemingly innocuous request. In the age of cell phones and watches, there is absolutely no reason anyone should ask you for the time. The predator is using this to distract you while he closes the distance. At the same time, he is assessing you.
- A man offers to help you and is insistent after you decline the help. This process of engagement allows him to assess you while closing the distance.
- You return to your car and notice a van parked close to your vehicle. Profiling works. When was the last time you heard of someone getting abducted in a MINI Cooper? Abductions require privacy and vans. Larger SUVs also offer this. The proximity of a predator's vehicle to yours allows him to achieve surprise and close the distance. It also gives him access to immediate privacy.
- You are walking and notice someone standing. Perhaps he is looking agitated, clenching and unclenching his fists, shifting and fidgeting, or other body language that looks out of place. This is often the physical behavior of someone pumping themselves up to commit a crime or an attack. In any event, change your path (without turning your back).

- You are walking, and you notice someone who does not seem to belong.
- You are jogging, and you hear (because you are *not* wearing earphones) someone running up from behind you. Don't immediately assume this is another jogger about to pass. Turn and look. They are closing the distance; turn and face the threat. (If you are wrong, what does it matter?)
- You are walking or jogging, and you see a male loitering on or near the path. Appearance matters. What are they wearing? What are they doing? Where are their hands? When was the last time you heard of a woman attacked on a park jogging path by a man in a suit? Is it hard to see their face? Criminals tend to try and hide their identities. No one gets dressed by accident.

But given that man is the most efficient predator on the food chain, there are other, more insidious tactics that are harder to detect but should, by their character, trigger an alarm response. These could include:

- An inappropriate amount of rapport building. Being overly friendly and/or offering too many details are subtle strategies predators use to assess and manipulate their potential victim. This exchange allows for him to close the distance.
- Engaging in a mild verbal exchange to test their victim's reaction. This verbal exchange allows him to close the distance.
- A woman answers her doorbell, and a solicitor asks to speak to "the man of the house." This is a common tactic to determine if the woman is alone. Face-to-face with the woman of the house, he has closed the distance.
- Posing as an authority figure but not giving a fulsome explanation and not having all of the props one would

expect, like flashing a law enforcement badge but not having a police car or any other additional equipment. The engagement allows him to close the distance.

Spot the trend? A predator knows that to get what he wants from you, he must close the distance, and if you understand that, you stand a much better chance of mitigating the threat. Once you are within an arm's length, you are in danger.

MANIPULATION AND ASSESSMENT

Predators manipulate and assess their targets. They are masters at the manipulation aspect, but we should remember that all of us have manipulated to one degree or another repeatedly over the course of our lives. We may do it to motivate subordinates or coworkers (otherwise referred to as "leadership"). We do it in our personal lives to pursue love interests and relationships. We see it in sales and advertising. We see it in how our children interact with us to get what they want. We see it in how we raise our children to mold them into the type of person we hope they will become. It happens routinely in espionage and law enforcement. It is a part of the human condition.

The difference, of course, is that the predator is manipulating his target to place her in a position of vulnerability, which is often the aspect of the hunt that gives him the most pleasure. The unexpected man wearing the electric company uniform convinces the lady of the house that he needs to check a meter inside. The man with an apparent cast on his arm needs help loading his van. The man who insisted on helping you carry your groceries is now suddenly in your apartment. The man who professes to be an undercover officer asks you to get into his undercover vehicle. The man who hurries to catch up with you only to engage in a conversation about the weather. These predators are closing the distance while assessing you at the same time. Something about the target caught their attention and made that person stand out from the herd. The predator perceives a vulnerability or lack of awareness on the part of the target, possibly someone engrossed in their phone or wearing headphones, or a mother focused on putting their baby in the child seat in the rear of the car. In the moments the predator is engaged in conversation, he is rapidly assessing his target: Is she pliable? Can she be manipulated? Is the woman hesitant? Is she confident? Does she rebuff him forcefully? Is the location conducive to privacy? Can he get close to her? Can he touch her? Can he touch her without warning?

THE MOST DANGEROUS WEAPON OF ALL—THE HUMAN MIND

In 2003, Sergeant Marcus Young was an eighteen-year veteran of the police force when he heard the call over the radio about potential male and female shoplifters at a local Walmart. He had with him Julian Covella, a seventeen-year-old cadet doing a ride along, and Sergeant Young thought it might be a good experience for the young cadet to witness the arrest of a shoplifter. The female suspect was already being held by the store security officer, but the male had left after the detention of the female. Sergeant Young arrived and took the woman into custody. Walking toward the police vehicle, he asked her about her accomplice.

The security officer described the male suspect as having neck tattoos, and, in the back of his mind, Young registered that he might have spent time in jail and was probably a felon.

"Does your boyfriend have any weapons? Do I have to be concerned for my safety?" he asked.

"No," she replied, but the manner in which she answered caught his attention.

As he finished securing her in the rear of the police vehicle, he turned to find the male suspect, hands in his jacket pockets, walking with determination toward him.

Unbeknownst to Young at the time, the male suspect was thirty-five-year-old ex-con Neal Beckman. Beckman had spent most of his adult life in prison for crimes, including stabbing an elderly man to death during a robbery.

"Take your hands out of your pockets!" commanded Young.

"Why is she in there?" demanded Beckman.

"I said take your hands out of your pockets!" repeated Young with more urgency.

"Why?" Beckman asked as he closed the distance.

"Because I'm concerned for my safety. What do you have in your pockets?" shouted Young.

Now within arm's-length, Beckman stated, "I have a knife." And he started to draw his hand from his pocket.

Years of training kicked in, and Sergeant Young, an experienced martial artist, executed a knife disarm as Beckman's hand was coming out of the pocket. He heard the sound of the wrist cracking. But as that was happening, Beckman took a revolver out of his other pocket and shot Young at point blank range. The first round entered his cheek, and then Young was fighting for his life. Beckman emptied the remaining four rounds into him. Two rounds hit his body armor, one entered his right arm, and one entered his left side.

Brett Schott, the unarmed security guard, in an act of incredible bravery, attacked Beckman from the rear. Grabbing the revolver, he attempted to fire it into Beckman, but now the gun was empty. Beckman, still holding the hunting knife, transferred it to his right hand and stabbed Schott in the chest. As Schott sank to the ground, Beckman ran toward the patrol car and frantically attempted to get the officer's long gun from inside the patrol vehicle. Schott, out of the fight and battling shock and blood loss, started to crawl away.

Young was on his knees. He was bleeding profusely, and his right arm was useless. His left hand had a two-inch tear between his index and middle finger. Seeing that Beckman was attempting to retrieve the long gun, Sergeant Young called out to Covella, the ride-along cadet who had taken cover between cars when the shots rang out, and directed him to come over and pull Young's sidearm from its holster and put it in his left hand. To his great credit, the young man did exactly that, albeit with some tense moments as he was struggling to free the firearm from its holster. After what must have felt like a lifetime, he freed the weapon from the holster and succeeded in placing it in Young's injured left hand.

His first two shots went into the passenger door directly where Beckman was, but the rounds did not penetrate the door. The shots did serve to alert Beckman, however, who redoubled his efforts to get at the long gun. Young then aimed through the glass and fired two more shots, and Beckman was down. The world was instantly a better place.

In an amazing feat of self-awareness, Sergeant Young realized that because he was bleeding profusely, he needed to lower his heart rate and focused on controlling his breathing as he waited for first responders to arrive.

This incident, which took place in a matter of seconds, reflects great heroism on behalf of Sergeant Young, Brett Schott, and the young Julian Covella (who definitely experienced the mother of all ride alongs). It also demonstrated the predatory mindset of the sociopath. Beckman willingly gave up his left hand with the knife as a ploy in order to get close enough to use his .38 revolver with his right hand. And the solution to this problem? Turn off the predator's brain. Turn off his brain, and whatever he was holding in his hand becomes a moot point.

Figure 4. Citizen Beckman gave up the knife in his left hand as a ploy to shoot a snub-nosed .38 with his right. Sergeant Young, however, achieved the optimal solution with two well-aimed shots.

PROXIMITY AND PRIVACY—EQUATES TO DEATH AND INJURY

Proximity is key. Anyone who is going to do you harm will do so within arm's length or closer. If they have a firearm or other weapon, that range could be extended by a couple of feet, but even then, they will want to be as close to you as possible. The predator wants and needs privacy to commit his act, and therefore, he will want to be out of the public eye to the extent possible. That could be a restroom, your home, an automobile, park path, or anywhere else that fits the purpose.

For the most part, we can largely control where we go. And if you don't like what you see, don't go there. How many women in an office building see the elevator door open to reveal a lone male occupant inside? And even if that occupant makes the woman feel uncomfortable, in the split-second decision to get on or not, more likely than not, she will get on. After all, it would be rude not to.

And as parents, this brings us to an interesting dichotomy in how we raise our children, especially our daughters. On the one hand, we want children to exhibit courtesy and politeness as they navigate the social spectrum. But on the other, we must empower them to say no and not worry about hurting a man's feelings. If that elevator door opens, and she doesn't like what she sees, by all means, we want her to listen to her instincts and pass on that elevator. Who cares if she trounces some fragile male egos or is occasionally deemed rude along the way? Better safe than the alternative.

By the same token, children must be guided from an early age in how to deal with strangers, but perhaps even more importantly, about how to deal with an adult or another child who makes them feel uncomfortable, even if that person is a relative or family friend. Abusive relatives can be particularly difficult to contend with, as parents may feel reluctant to press an issue or report it to the authorities either out of shame or family equities. Growing up, most children are taught to be polite to adults. This is not entirely correct. Yes, be polite with all people, but if something feels wrong, they must remove themselves from the situation and have enough faith in their parents to tell them. All adults do not deserve respect. Difficult? Yes. But then, anyone who is already a parent knows that being a parent is the hardest job in the world and the one job that carries more responsibility than any other job they will ever have.

A second consideration to remember is if the predator takes you to a secondary location, you will almost certainly be brutalized and killed. Your chance of survival is exponentially greater if you stand and fight with everything you have because once you are in a private location of your abductor's choosing, the odds of surviving the experience are severely diminished. Your own home could constitute that secondary location. The bottom line is that he will need a place that affords him privacy. If you go to his space, the chances of you suffering greatly is certain. This really boils down to "Don't get taken alive." This lesson was seared into my psyche early in my agency career during a training iteration.

We were training to undergo interrogation. In the days leading up to the actual training event, we were prepped on how to prepare. A psychologist told us about the physical and mental challenges we could expect to encounter. Interrogation methods were discussed. Strategies for resistance were reviewed. We just didn't know when the event would occur, as it was embedded in other concurrent paramilitary training. Sure enough, after a couple of days of field problems when we were already tired and worn out, we heard the sound of gunfire, the door to the open bay barracks burst open, and masked assailants firing AKs entered. We were herded outside, hoods were placed on our heads, and we were put in vans for transport to some unknown location. At that location, we were forced out again into the woods and made to crawl through muddy, stagnant water, all the while being abused by the guards. Finally, we were walked over to the holding facility, cuffed and smelling of swamp mud. And that was just the beginning.

There then ensued two days and nights of interrogations. Between interrogations, we were forced to stand up, always with the dirty hoods over our eyes and faces. Some were moved to small boxes for minor infractions. It didn't take long to lose track of time, meanwhile always standing. Some of the rooms had hot lights. We could hear interrogations taking place with yelling by the guards and sounds of bodies hitting the walls. The sleep deprivation created a dreamlike state. Years later, the Obama administration put restrictions on how prisoners in the global war on terror could be treated. I had to laugh, as what we put our own officers (and soldiers who undergo similar training in escape and evasion) through was much more severe than the way Taliban and ISIS militants could be treated. Moreover, we publicized our procedures to the world, and make no mistake, our enemies know what our limitations are. Brilliant.

In any event, the standing and waiting was so agonizing that after a while, I actually looked forward to the interrogations, as it would break up the monotony of standing in a room hooded and under hot lights. Some trainees started to hallucinate as the hours went by and sleep deprivation took its toll. Eventually, we were rescued when a force assaulted the jail and liberated us (which I recall I was reluctant to believe as I couldn't discount the possibility that it was a false-flag rescue).

It was an excellent training evolution, and each trainee definitely learned something about themselves, and it burned two lessons into me: know you cover story and don't get taken alive. The latter was because the training exemplified that people can be excruciatingly cruel, even in a controlled training environment that only lasted a couple of days. It was an extremely hard experience. I can only marvel with complete admiration how people like John McCain and other American POWs survived so many years of real physical and mental torture at the hands of their North Vietnamese captors.

Don't get taken alive. That advice is equally appropriate for women facing a potentially violent situation. Don't get taken to a secondary location. This goes against traditional advice, which advocates compliance to stay alive. History has shown that going to a secondary location is overwhelmingly likely to result in a brutal death.

But in order to guard against a threat, you have to acknowledge that one exists. You have to accept the fact that truly evil persons exist in our world, that they thrive on the thrill of the hunt, that they derive power from holding a life in their hands, that they know how to use violence to their advantage, and that they know in order to do that, they must get close to you in order to execute their plan with overwhelming violence and surprise.

Conversely, we can also accept that predators don't have to be the only ones to use intelligence, guile, and sudden violence. The average person can learn, through training and forethought, how to unleash violence in the same manner as the sociopath: without mercy and with cold precision. This course of action begins with improving our situational awareness. Learning to look for potential problems will mitigate most problems. It also includes understanding that when we are caught by surprise, we will experience denial, deliberation, and hopefully, meaningful action, and that meaningful action is more likely to occur if we give a potential problem forethought. We'll look at practical measures of walking the streets, defending our home, and the pros and cons of weapons. Then we can look at physical options about how to break another human being.

KEY CONCEPTS

- Predators exhibit indicators—sometimes subtle and sometimes brazen. Accept that there are evil persons among us who have zero empathy for another human being.
- A predator must be close to you to do you harm, literally within arm's reach. Watch for verbal ploys ("Excuse me, do you have the time?"), especially when you are in a vulnerable place, like a parking lot or city park.
- The predator enjoys the hunt. He manipulates and assesses his target. Maintain situational awareness. Unsolicited approaches, insistence on helping, and not accepting "no" should trigger alarms.
- Don't go to the secondary location of the predator's choosing. If you do, you will almost certainly be killed.
- If you feel uneasy about a situation, take action. Better to hurt someone's feelings or have them wonder about your intent than to become a victim. Don't worry about being deemed rude or allow someone to make you feel that way.
- When it comes to defending yourself, fight like a sociopath: without empathy or mercy. Think about how to do this; learn how to do this.
- When we are caught by surprise in a violent situation, we can expect to go through a series of emotions that starts with denial, then deliberation, and finally action. For some, this could last fractions of a second, or for others, much longer. Some may never get to action. We can mitigate the debilitating effects of sudden violence through forethought and planning, and in physical violence, through practice of combative and defensive measures.

5

PROTECTING OUR CHILDREN AND SITUATIONAL AWARENESS

WOLVES—LARGE AND SMALL

Clearly the aforementioned predators constitute an obvious threat to our children. But what about child-on-child crime? Gavin de Becker, in his book *Protecting the Gift*, provides a stunning example of child-on-child sexual assault and a school's complete failure to address the problem. In one instance, a young male was accused of sexually assaulting another male student in the restroom. The family of the victim sued the school. At trial, the defense attempted to suggest that the sex was consensual, except the defense conveniently glossed over the fact that the student had done the same thing a month earlier with another child in the same bathroom. Worse, the previous school the young male child attended had reported to the current school the following pattern of behavior (remember that past behavior is the best predictor of future behavior):

- He carried a knife.
- He threatened to kill.
- He threatened and attempted suicide.
- He had a fascination with fire.
- He poured gasoline on his mother and attempted to light it.
- He engaged in inappropriate sexual conduct toward other children.

This child aggressor was ten years old. Ten. And the school's reaction to the first assault? Well, the principal decided that the problem child should have an escort when he went to the restroom. And in a moment of brilliance, this highly paid public official who oversaw the education and safety of the children decided the escort would be—another child! The school district rightfully lost its case. But what kind of adult do you imagine this child aggressor will become?

So when your child goes to someone's home to play, ask yourself the following rhetorical questions: Do you know everything about the parents, the friend, and any siblings? Do other people frequent the house? Do you know if there are guns in the house and how they are stored? Are the children supervised? Does one of the parents have anger issues? An arrest record? A drinking problem? How about the other kids in the house? Is there anything in the background of one of the members of the family that would cause you concern? Do you allow yourself to feel better because one of the adult members of the household is a veteran, a doctor, a church member, a volunteer clown, a chocolate factory worker, a former police officer, or a suicide hotline volunteer?

Let's look at an intelligence community paradigm. To be accepted into the Central Intelligence Agency, you must pass a host of hurdles, including the extensive application itself, detailed background investigations, psychological testing, multiple interviews, batteries of tests, and polygraph examinations. Moreover, the checking and testing is continuous throughout your career. And yet, even with the overwhelming scrutiny and checks, there are still a small number of employees who engage in illegal or criminal behavior. These crimes range from misappropriation of funds to assault and battery and everything in between. Add to the mix employees who are fired for security issues, such as not reporting foreign contacts, or in the worst possible case, conducting espionage against the United States. While these events are extremely rare, they still happen. So even in an otherwise elite and squeaky-clean population, there is still a certain percentage of people who engage in illicit activities and deviant behaviors. The good news about the CIA is that these persons are almost certainly found out eventually. In the Marine Corps we used to say that no matter how elite a unit, there is always that 10 percent who bring down the reputation and performance of the organization. So if that 10 percent rule applies to elite units, what about your neighborhood?

All of this is not to say that we should walk through life avoiding contact with other human beings. But what it should strongly suggest to you is that you should increase your level of awareness about everyone around you and your family. It's obvious when you are at the ATM withdrawing funds, but it's less obvious when you are at the neighborhood picnic with your kids, a church function, a local sports club, or have contractors working in your home. It's not so obvious, too, when you are putting your faith in the school system and others to take appropriate action to protect your child.

STRATEGIES FOR KEEPING OUR CHILDREN SAFE

There are some simple strategies you can use with your children to help keep them safe:

- **Play the "what if" game.** Whenever we go somewhere with the children, I ask them, "Hey, if a bad guy came into the store with a gun or something, where should we go?" This immediately gets them to look for a rear exit. They have fun, and it's not alarming to them. At the same time, they are learning to hone their awareness.
- **Rally point.** Also, if we go to a mall or large public place like an amusement park, we always pick a place where we can rally if we get separated. This has to be an obvious landmark that they can remember and find. Fortunately, we've never had to test this methodology, but if we do, it's better to have a plan in place.
- **Asking for help.** If they can't find the landmark, then their next course of action is to *ask a woman* for help as recommended by Gavin de Becker. Why? The vast preponderance of sex offenders and predators are men, and a woman is more likely to help the child to a satisfactory conclusion. I tell my children to "find a woman who looks like a mom."
- **Easy to see.** Dress your little ones in colorful clothing that will make it easy for you to track their movements. Just go to a kids' park on a weekend, and you will understand how quickly you can lose sight of them. In the same vein, you should dress in something that is easy for the child to see.
- **Passwords.** Have a password for your children. Tell them that they should never go with anyone unless that person knows the password, and under no circumstances should they reveal it. This has to be approached with some tact so as not to scare the child, but at the same time, it needs to be revisited frequently to ingrain it into the child's psyche.

- **Threats.** Teach your children to never heed threats. For example, if an adult or other child does something with them (read "sexual assault") and then says something to the effect of "Don't tell, or I will kill your parents," they should absolutely tell you. Assure them that this is a trick bad people use and that they should tell you immediately. More importantly, your children must feel that they can come to you for any reason (that would be a book unto itself) and not worry about the consequences.
- **Teach them to be rude** (if the situation warrants it). If they feel uncomfortable about someone, it's OK to be rude and refuse to ride, walk, or stay with a person who makes them feel this way. More often than not, it will be someone known to the family. Sadly, this could include relatives. Encourage them to talk to you if someone makes them feel anxious, even if it's a friend or relative.
- **Cars.** When you are putting your kids in the car and are busy getting them buckled in, tell your child (in a playful way) for them to let you know if they see an adult behind you. Even a tenth of a second of advanced warning that something is amiss is better than none at all.
- **Sleepovers.** Avoid sending your children on sleepovers. Better to host them than to possibly place your children at risk.

ACT ON YOUR INSTINCTS

When it comes to traversing daily life or taking care of your children, be attuned to your instincts. If something makes you uneasy, listen to your instincts and, more importantly, have the courage to act on them. For example, if you are a woman, and the door to the elevator opens, and you see a man in there who gives you pause, don't get on. If you are hesitant to go into a poorly lit and deserted garage, don't go in. If you are walking down the street, and you see someone standing there who makes you uneasy, cross the street or turn around. If you see an adult talking to your child in a manner that makes you uneasy, take your child. Don't ignore it! Teach your children to be polite, but let them know that is OK to be rude if an adult makes them uncomfortable. But now, here comes the caveat.

The hard part about this—as the victims of the aforementioned killers learned—is that, often, you don't identify the true predator until it's too late. Way too late. Why is that? Is it because they cloak themselves in a semblance of normalcy? Or is it because we talk ourselves out of believing there could be danger? Or maybe our state of awareness is not what it should be. The answer is, yes, usually it's a combination of all of these.

SITUATIONAL AWARENESS

At the CIA, we highly regard an officer who is considered to be "situationally aware." What does that mean, and how can you cultivate it? Situational awareness is simply being in a higher-than-normal state of alert. It is looking for potential problems on the street, in the subway, when going to and from our cars, at the bar, in the taxi, on the bus, at the grocery store; in fact, there really is no end to it. Pretty easy, right? Wrong. It's mentally exhausting. You simply cannot be in a high state of situational awareness all of the time. There have been times in my life when I was more situationally aware for extended periods, such as in war zones or in particularly dangerous locales. So it would make sense to say that there are degrees of awareness. When I am at home, that is logically where I am the most relaxed. I don't need to check my family member's hands for weapons or look at how someone is standing or assess if they are paying attention to me in my home. When I open the door to walk toward my car, the situational awareness starts to ramp up. Working in the counterterrorism realm for as many years as I did, I understand that two potential choke points for me as a target are in the vicinity of my home and my workplace. I will eventually always end up there. Depending on where I am in the world, I might check my car to look for signs of tampering (explosives) before I get in and start the ignition. As I drive, I start to scan the road, looking for signs that something is not normal. This could be other cars, people loitering, or objects along the road that weren't there before. This is the state of being situationally aware. I'm not singing along with Robert Plant on "Stairway to Heaven" or chatting with my wife on the speaker phone. Rather, my focus is on everything around me. I basically know what is normal for the environment I am traversing, so I ignore that which is normal. Rather, I am looking for anything that looks different, something that does not belong.

When I'm in a city environment, the same thing applies from the moment I step out of my hotel room. I am scanning and assessing people I see in the hall and elevator. I can still greet people and be a normal human being, but the assessment is continuous. How are they dressed? Where are their hands? Is there anything in their demeanor that causes pause? On the street, this awareness goes higher. Does anyone seem to be paying undue attention to me? When I enter the subway, I am not engaged on the phone, and I don't listen to music. I stand on the platform, where I can see and hear everything around me. If someone causes me to pause, I keep my distance. On the train ride, I pick a spot where I can see most, if not all, of the train car. I am aware of everything happening around me. I identify people who cause concern and keep them in my periphery. If I have real concerns about someone, I might change train cars or get off and get the next train. This can sound like a lot of effort.

In a way, it's like Zen meditation. Think you can sit quietly and take ten deep breaths without your mind wandering? The short answer is no, you can't. Your mind will wander. It will shock you just how much. Over time and experience, however, you will be able to sit calmly for longer periods of time as the thoughts ebb and flow. And so it is with situational awareness. You don't have to walk around in a state of paranoia. That would defeat the purpose. But you can make it a habit to simply start paying attention to what is around you. Common sense dictates that in a more dangerous environment, you ratchet up your level of awareness. So situational awareness can help us when we journey among strangers.

Understand, too, that you cannot always maintain this level of awareness. You need to be able to turn it on and off to be effective and to maintain your mental health. The inability to ratchet down from a higher state of awareness can lead to post-traumatic stress disorder (PTSD)—a not uncommon affliction of soldiers or marines who have been in a continuous state of high awareness during a deployment. They are in such a high state that, over time, it impacts their ability to sleep and, ultimately, to handle the frustrations and challenges of daily life.

So start the challenge of increasing your awareness as you traverse the planet. You will find that you will get better at it quickly, and within a short amount of time, you will start to do it without thinking about it. In a similar vein, assess people.

You've done this most of your life anyway without realizing it. But now do it within the framework of keeping yourself and your children safe. As with situational awareness, you will improve quickly and in short order.

Children deserve and need the most protection in society. Threats to them usually come from adults, but they can come from children as well. Raise your level of awareness for their circumstances as the situation dictates. A threat is a threat, and man is, above all other creatures, the most cunning and dangerous beast in the jungle.

KEY CONCEPTS

- Be wary of strangers for sure, but increase your awareness of those you know. Take a look beneath the veneer—a good look.
- You have almost no way of really knowing other people's inner behaviors short of living with them, and even then, that is no guarantee. Look at how many serial killers were "family men." Therefore, don't let your children go on sleepovers. Better to invite their friends to your home. That may seem overly protective, but it's better to be safe than sorry.
- Understand that there is such a thing as child-on-child assault. Don't depend on institutions or other families to always take appropriate action in the interests of child safety.
- When you take your children to a public place, have them wear distinctive clothing that will easily allow you to track their movements. Do the same so they can find you just as easily.
- Have a password for your children so that if an adult ever

comes to them—friend or stranger—they should know the password. If not, teach your child not to go with them. This has to be reviewed and practiced to ingrain it into your children's routine. It should stand without saying that you should not reveal the password to someone who does not have the need to know.

- Play the "what if" game with your kids. Every time you go somewhere with them, ask them, "What if something bad were to happen, where would we go?"
- Have a rally point. Wherever we go, I always tell my children that if we get separated, for whatever reason, we should meet up at location X. This is usually a highly visible landmark. This works in malls, theme parks, etc.
- Again, Gavin de Becker offers excellent advice: if a child must ask someone for help, better to *ask a woman*. This is not to say that a woman cannot be a kidnapper, but the odds favor the child to ask a woman for help rather than a man, as a woman will likely see the problem through to a conclusion, that is, get the child to the proper authorities.
- Predators rely on surprise to gain proximity to their target. So it stands to reason that if a target is in a higher state of awareness prior to the encounter, they can potentially mitigate the danger.
- Cultivate your situational awareness but understand that you can't be in a state of high awareness 100 percent of the time. Know when to employ it and know how to ratchet it back. Practice. Before long, it will imprint into your DNA.
- Assess people within the framework of the safety for yourself and for your family.
- Teach your children to be polite but also to not be afraid to be rude if they feel uncomfortable with someone. Encourage them to talk to you if anyone—even a family friend or a relative—makes them feel uncomfortable. They should

definitely tell you if anyone threatens violence against the family if they tell someone about an incident.

6

ASSAULT, DATE RAPE, CHINESE DRUGS, AND INTERVENTIONS

WOMEN: THE MOST AT-RISK SEGMENT OF SOCIETY

Within twenty-four hours of reading this, about 140 women across the globe will be murdered. Most will be killed by someone they know. This is the average number of women murdered on a daily basis. Some estimates suggest that 150,000 of the more than 180,000 women killed annually are killed by an intimate partner or former intimate partner. If any segment of society is at greater risk than others, it would be that of young women aged twelve to twenty-three. And of that group, perhaps the midteens are at the greatest risk. These are young women who are entering various stages of sexual and emotional maturity. They are starting to become attuned to the influence and attention their femininity can garner in society. The teen years (as just about everyone who has survived them can attest) also tend to be the years where young people take the greatest risks socially and physically. Moreover, a teenage girl is more likely than most segments of society to avoid reporting a sexual assault due to embarrassment, parental issues, or peer pressure. She is, by her very nature, of keen interest to a predator.

In a similar vein, the elderly and disabled are also at high risk to falling victim to crime, assault, and financial manipulation. It's difficult to imagine that as a civilized species, so much suffering is imposed on the women and elders in our midst, but it is.

The National Intimate Partner and Sexual Violence Survey (NISVS) for 2010 to 2012 indicated that approximately one in five women in the U.S. experienced rape at some point in their life, and according to RAINN (Rape, Abuse & Incest National Network), a sexual assault occurs about once every ninety-two seconds. Furthermore, they estimate that an astounding 34 percent of victims of sexual assault and rape are under age twelve, and that 66 percent of victims are between twelve and eighteen years of age.

Some additional statistics of concern:

- About 48 percent were sleeping or at home.
- 29 percent were traveling to and from work or school, or on their way to shop or run errands.
- 12 percent were working.
- 7 percent were attending school.
- 5 percent were engaged in an activity, such as exercise.

Keep in mind that most sexual assaults are done by people known to the victim. Even the rich and famous are not immune, as exemplified by TV personality Ellen DeGeneres, who was victimized by her stepfather at age fifteen when her mother was diagnosed with breast cancer. The stepfather pressured her repeatedly for him to conduct a breast examination. And as so often is the case, her mother took years to finally believe Ellen's account of events.

DATE RAPE

Tina enjoyed going to the hotel nightclub on her night off with her friends. It was reputed to be one of the best clubs in the city. The live band was always good, and ladies' night promotions always offered deeply discounted drinks. The latter point didn't matter much to her, as she generally would sip on a cola and dance the night away with her friends. The ladies dressed to impress, and there were always interesting people.

That night, like most of the others, she showed her ID to get in, and as the doors opened, the cloud of cigarette smoke literally billowed into the entranceway. The sound of the live band made conversation a challenge, but you could feel a vibrancy to the music. As usual, the club was standing room only. Tina saw two of her female work colleagues at a standing side table, and she ordered a cola from the bar. Within a short time, she and her friends had joined the throng of people near the front of the stage dancing.

During one of the band's breaks, Tina and her friends were approached by a man—a customary occurrence for these attractive young ladies. The man, who introduced himself as Peter, seemed charming and engaged Tina in casual banter. Tina wasn't particularly interested in Peter, but she didn't want to be rude. As the band started up again, Tina's friends went back to the dance floor, leaving her with Peter. Seeing that her drink was low, Peter offered to refresh it for her. Tina declined, but Peter insisted, invoking his mother, who would surely chastise him if she knew he were not being a gentleman. Tina relented. A short time later, Peter made his way through the throng of dancers with the drink in hand.

About twenty minutes later, Tina started to feel dizzy. To her surprise, she heard herself slurring her words a bit. Stating that the smoke and loud music were taking a toll, Peter suggested they step out into the hotel lobby for some fresher air and a quieter location.

But once in the lobby, she still felt sleepy and found coordination difficult, almost as if she were drunk. Expressing alarm for her condition, Peter offered—somewhat insistently—to drive her home. Unable to think clearly, she accepted, and they made their way to the car. As soon as she entered the car, she felt an overwhelming urge to sleep.

Several hours later, she woke up to the sound of running feet. As she opened her eyes, she had no idea where she was or how she came to be in the quiet park. The feet she heard were those of two early-morning joggers. Tina was disheveled and had unexplained cuts and scrapes on her legs. Her panties were in a heap some meters away. She felt pain in and around her vagina, and she realized with horror that she had been sexually assaulted.

She had no recollection of what had transpired the previous six hours. Confused and crying, she simply could not piece together what had happened. The shame she felt was immeasurable. She had always considered herself savvy and smart, yet this had happened to her. How could she explain it? Who could she tell? What would her friends and parents think?

She didn't know it, but that last cola she drank contained Rohypnol, otherwise known as "the date rape drug." Rohypnol belongs to a family of medication called benzodiazepine, which includes the likes of such medications as Valium, Librium, and Xanax. Illegal in the U.S., it is widely available in Mexico, South America, Europe, and Asia as a sleep aid for insomnia.

Like Rohypnol, gamma-hydroxybutyrate (GHB) is clear and odorless. It comes in liquid, powder, tablet, and capsule forms. Street names include: Grievous Bodily Harm, G, Liquid Ecstasy, and Georgia Home Boy.* GHB is popular at nightclubs and raves and can be manufactured in home labs from recipes obtained on the internet. Effects can last three to four hours. Legally manufactured GHB is approved for treating narcolepsy in the U.S. and is tightly restricted.

A third type of prevalent rape drug is ketamine, an anesthetic used in veterinary medicine and as an emergency anesthetic for humans. The effects can last thirty to sixty minutes. China is the epicenter of illegal ketamine production. The low cost of ketamine there has taken a terrible toll in the form of addiction across all segments of society. In 2013, the Chinese government undertook a large crackdown on ketamine and methamphetamine production. In Guangdong Province, Chinese authorities conducted, in essence, a large-scale military-type operation against illegal labs in the town of Boshe. In the early morning hours, more than 3,000 police descended on the town. The Communist leader of the town was arrested and later executed. For years, authorities tried to raid the town, but at each attempt, the drug barons had

---

* https://archives.drugabuse.gov/publications/nida-community-drug-alert-bulletin-club-drugs/gamma-hydroxybutyrate-ghb

advanced warning through their sources within the Communist Party.

While Communist authorities succeeded in disrupting drug production in Boshe, they did not succeed in eliminating the ketamine production problem. Chinese drug makers simply started to set up production elsewhere in China and expanded into Cambodia, Thailand, Myanmar, and Malaysia.

Given the transnational threat to regional security and U.S. interests, it might surprise some in the public to know that the CIA collects intelligence and works with liaison partners around the globe to combat drug production and drug smuggling. I worked this issue in Southeast Asia for three years and saw firsthand the successes and failures of partner nations dealing with this corrosive issue in their midst. Emerging economies, such as Cambodia, are ill-equipped to deal with this kind of social plague. To be sure, law enforcement in Southeast Asia has had some significant victories, but clearly, the problem is daunting, and the forces arrayed against drugs in these countries is largely underfunded and understaffed. Moreover, most law enforcement entities are interested in arrest statistics to demonstrate success. With pressure to get arrests and convictions, the result, more often than not, is that only lower-level drug lords are arrested, while the real masterminds and financial kingpins remain largely unmolested.

While I only worked this issue for three years, I was impressed at the efforts of some highly dedicated host-nation officers in these countries. As one counterpart mentioned to me, "It's not easy to be conducting surveillance on a drug lord, watching the lifestyle he is living—the money, fancy cars, and women— when we are sitting in surveillance vehicles wondering how we are going to manage our bills that month." These are the silent warriors of our times, and I give a grateful thanks to them and to our brothers in the Drug Enforcement Administration, who give up so much in blood, sweat, and tears to prosecute the counternarcotic mission. Given the impact that illegal drugs have on our society, one could quite convincingly argue that this impact far outweighs the threat of terrorism on our shores. It is directly responsible for untold violence and misery in our times and is therefore a direct threat to our national interests. In my humble opinion, people engaged in the drug trade should be dealt with as harshly as the Taliban, al Qaeda, or the Haqqani network leader. Just saying...

Drugs represent a modern-day twist to the danger posed by men against women in society, and they are generally administered surreptitiously by strangers to their targets. But violence against women is more likely to be executed by someone known to the victim than by a stranger.

In any given week, the news headlines are replete with the murders of women by men. In a rare instance when a man is killed by a woman, it is usually because she was defending herself from abuse. Victims span all ages and nationalities. For example, during this writing, headlines for one week revealed that a molecular biologist was hit by a man in his car—twice—and then dragged off into a private location and raped. A seventy-seven-year-old man was convicted of stabbing a woman to death in front of her children—the same way he murdered his wife forty years prior. A woman and her boyfriend were murdered on a lonely stretch of highway in Canada. A seventy-two-year-old woman was shot to death by her husband. A Navy airman was arrested for paying an undercover officer to kill his wife for $500.

The threats of violence a woman faces, from acquaintance and stranger alike, are extensive and varied. That men are aggressors against women in societies across the globe, there is no doubt. That we should raise our sons to respect women, there is no doubt. But wishing it will not make it so. And what is so painful about the endless list of statistics and incidents is that for the women victims, a little bit of knowledge about how to injure a man could have affected the outcomes of many situations.

INTERVENTIONS—CHOOSE CAREFULLY

Ask any police officer, and he or she will tell you that the most dangerous type of response for an officer is a domestic disturbance call. Emotions are highly charged. Since firearms are readily available throughout American society, it is no coincidence that more police officers are killed in the line of duty for this kind of call than any other.

Standing on the subway platform, I noticed the movement in my peripheral vision. A young black couple in their early twenties or late teens was sitting on one of the benches. There were only a handful of riders waiting for the midday train. The young woman made a sudden move as if to run up the stairs, but her companion grabbed her arm and forced her to sit down next to him. It was clear some kind of argument was taking place and that the man was exerting physical pressure—not overly obvious but pressure nonetheless. It caught my attention, and I started to watch, and this is where a moral dilemma started to percolate.

Who were these people? What was the argument? What was the relationship? Was he holding her against her will? They seemed well dressed, but did he have a weapon? What was his intent? He had the physique of an athlete—not that it matters when you crush a throat, rupture a testicle, or take out an eye—but it could have a bearing on everything leading up to those last resorts.

As the trains in that city never run on time, the drama started to unfold as the low-volume argument between the couple continued. She tried a couple of times to get up, but the man would grab her arm and have her sit next to him each time.

At this point, a young professional-looking white woman started to take an interest. I knew instantly that as a woman, she was concerned about a domestic abuse issue taking place. She asked the woman if she was all right. The woman responded affirmatively, but the argument continued.

Suddenly, the black woman broke free and ran up the stairs toward the ticket master booth. The man followed. I could hear the volume of their argument getting louder. I figured if anything transpired, the ticket master in his contained booth would call authorities. (Again, wrong assumption.) But now, the young white woman followed up the stairs. And for me, the moral dilemma compounded, particularly as I have a daughter around the same age as the two women.

Resigning myself, up the stairs I went, running over in my mind various options. I had an improvised weapon in the form of a magazine, and I knew what targets on the body I would go for if it came to it (eyes, throat, groin, and possibly an ankle or knee after he was distracted with another injury). When I arrived at the top, the man was still holding the woman by the arm. The white woman was videoing the struggle with her phone and the man was growing increasingly angry—at his partner and at the interfering woman.

While I am technically challenged, the prospect of instant notoriety and evidence through social media immediately struck me as a good idea, and so I took out my phone and started doing the same thing. The young man grew increasingly frustrated but now recognized that he was on the horns of a dilemma with two people videoing him. Then to my surprise, the young black woman announced everything was OK, and she went down a different staircase to a different platform with her partner in tow. Whatever happened after that is anyone's guess, although I'd stake my life on it not ending well for her.

The young white woman and I returned to our platform and boarded the train a moment later. She was shaking and teary. I complimented her for her actions and explained that she was feeling the aftereffects of the adrenaline. She could barely respond, so strong were her emotions at the moment.

That kind of intervention could have ended any number of ways, most of them not pleasant. The young man could have escalated the confrontation with a weapon, placing all involved at risk of death or serious injury. The man might have initiated a physical confrontation short of deadly force. He might have initiated a physical confrontation that resulted in death inadvertently because once a violent encounter begins, there is no real control as to how the encounter will end. He might have initiated a physical confrontation that could have ended his life if he underestimated an older man...

We were lucky that day. I don't know about the woman we

were concerned about. Most likely, she was trapped in a relationship that she did not know how to get out of. Like millions of women across the globe, she likely felt outmatched physically and intimidated psychologically. If only she possessed the knowledge to know she could even the playing field against a bigger, faster, and stronger opponent. A pity, as such knowledge is definitely within her grasp.

FIGHTING BACK

Murder, sexual assault, domestic abuse—our daughters, sisters, and mothers suffer it more than any other segment of society. But there are ways to fight back. Even a little knowledge can go a long way. And while ultimately knowing how to break another human body is within the grasp of women of all ages, it is not the physical ability alone that will allow you to traverse the dangers of the modern world. The physical strategies should be coupled with situational awareness, common sense, and importantly, the will to win. We will look at some preemptive strategies for walking the street and measures to protect your home. We will look at the pros and cons of various weapons and, finally, how to employ some physical strategies with only your hands so that in the unfortunate event the universe should choose to align its stars against you, you will prevail. The will to win? That must come from within.

KEY CONCEPTS

- Date-rape drugs are a real and present danger to women in societies across the globe. Be aware of the existence of these drugs and their effects. *Never* leave your drink unattended. If you do, toss it and get another.

- Remember that your level of awareness will decrease with increased alcohol intake.
- Don't give in to peer pressure.
- If you ever do think that you have been victimized by one of these drugs, report it. Traces of Rohypnol dissipate after about seventy-two hours, GHB after about five hours, and ketamine after about forty-eight hours, according to the Office on Women's Health (womenshealth.gov).
- Women and young teens age twelve to twenty-three constitute the most at-risk segment of the female population.
- Assaults against women by strangers are the ones that capture our attention the most. No doubt this constitutes a clear danger. At the same time, keep in mind that most assaults are conducted by someone known to the victim. Former and current boyfriends and husbands rank highest on the list as abusers.
- A little knowledge on how to damage the human body could alter the outcome for a significant percentage of violent attacks against women.
- Couple physical skills with situational awareness and some commonsense measures to give you the greatest chance of success.
- Cultivate your will to win—no matter the circumstances— so that you will prevail in the worst fifteen seconds of the worst day of your life.

7

TAKING IT TO THE STREET

AWARENESS, CRIME, AND CONTINGENCY PLANNING

If we look at the FBI's crime statistics for an average American city like Richmond, Virginia, we can see that in the first six months of 2018, there were 559 reported violent crimes, 26 murders, 27 rapes, 194 robberies, 312 aggravated assaults, 4,125 property crimes, 475 burglaries, 3,073 larceny-thefts, 577 motor vehicle thefts, and 23 arsons. Keep in mind that these are only cases that were reported by the victims, classified by local law enforcement officials, and reported by those agencies. The actual numbers are likely much higher (and this is just for six months). If we just look at the numbers of property crimes and burglaries alone, we can see that if you lived in Richmond, you would have good cause for concern.

In considering self-protection measures, you will never be able to think of every contingency, but you can look at your routines, identify the places where you are most likely at risk, and develop a contingency plan for it. Consider your commute to work. Where you park. Where you shop and how you get to those locales. Think about people you routinely interact with, where you bank, and what pharmacies you frequent. And then you can start to play the "what if" game. What if you were in Costco and suddenly heard shots ring out? What would you do? I think we could all agree that the moment of truth is not the ideal time to decide. So instead, every time you enter a place, ask yourself that question. And if your answer to your higher awareness self is "I would go to the rear exit," then make sure you identify where that is. If, for whatever reason, that alternate exit is not available, then identify a secondary location where you could go. I do this now habitually. It only takes a few seconds of thought, and I can then refocus on the mundane task that took me there. It doesn't matter if it's a movie theater or a grocery store, I locate the alternate exit.

In general, under stress, people default to their level of training. If you have undergone firearms training in the last fifteen years, you have probably heard about the police officer who was tragically killed in a shoot-out with a suspect, and later, it was discovered that the officer had empty shells in his pocket, meaning that in a moment of stress, he had picked up his spent shells from the ground. Why? That was the way he trained. The range rules were meticulous about picking up your brass. In his moment of greatest need, he defaulted to his training and picked up the spent brass.

WALKING THE WALK

When my oldest son was accepted into an inner-city university, he was excited at the prospect of newfound freedom and adventure of the variety that college affords. As a parent familiar with that city, I was less than enthusiastic. One day early on in his tenure, I grabbed him and said, "Come on, let's go for a walk." He was surprised. (It's not altogether bad to keep young adults in your family guessing.) We started walking the city blocks from his apartment toward the downtown campus. As we walked, I started to revisit the idea of sifting out the abnormal from the normal—situational awareness.

DON'T BE DEAF—DITCH THE EARPHONES

"First things first," I began, "never, under any circumstance, walk around with earphones." The animal kingdom is pretty brutal about natural selection, and everyone knows that the weakest animals are killed and eaten. In the human paradigm, why would you want to eliminate one of your greatest assets: your ability to hear? Don't believe me? Here is a challenge. Go to Google and type in "the knockout game" or "knockout" or "mugging." Up will come dozens of attacks caught on security cameras. The knockout game is particularly detestable. In this "game," the attacker comes up behind his victim and swings as hard as he can to the jaw/face of his victim who is caught completely unaware, often because they are listening to music or are focused on their phones. In addition to getting coldcocked out of the blue, the victim generally sustains an additional, sometimes life-ending, injury when they slip into unconsciousness and their head hits the pavement. In the high preponderance of these attacks, the predator runs up from behind the victim to achieve maximum surprise. Sociopaths, people who engage in this type of activity, lack any empathy for other human beings—a concept that is difficult for anyone who possesses even a modicum of empathy to comprehend.

Chances are, you know someone who fits the profile of a sociopath or close to it. They are predators, they are the wolves among us, and very often, they are difficult to discern until it's too late. If you hear running feet or a quickening of someone's pace, turn around and look! But you can't do that if you don't hear the sound of feet coming from behind. I recently saw a news story where the broadcaster solemnly advised at the end to "turn down the volume." Not good enough and not worth your life. Ditch the earphones and enjoy your music the other twenty-three hours of the day.

Predators are looking for easy prey. They want to maximize their chances of getting what they want. You are a resource to a predator. When he comes up behind you and initiates an onslaught of knife thrusts into you at the ATM, he is simply there to gather his resource. Why make it easier for a predator by having headphones on? Why deny yourself the second or fraction of a second you might need to have a fighting chance? Why stand out among the herd as a viable target?

And yet, go to any college campus and watch how many women jog with headphones. It is absolutely astounding.

Consider Anne (not her real name). In 2018, she went out as she normally did for a run. She was an experienced and dedicated runner. It was late afternoon, and she noticed two men walking toward her on the park path. She passed them, like so many others, without a second thought. Moments later, she pitched forward and lost her balance as one of them came up from behind and pushed her. As she was falling down, she felt an object against her cheek and heard an electric buzzing of the taser as it emptied a charge into her. Terrified and not understanding what was happening, she started to scream, apparently loud enough to cause her attacker to run away. She told the police that she never heard her attacker run up behind her. The reason? She was wearing earphones.

On April 19, 1989, a twenty-eight-year-old financial analyst named Trisha Meili was jogging in Central Park, New York City. She was wearing her headphones, listening to music, so she never heard her attacker run up behind her and tackle her to the ground. She was hit in the back of the head with something and dragged into the brush, where she was repeatedly struck with a rock and raped. Comatose for twelve days, she was not expected to survive. Against the odds she did survive, but her life was altered forever.

On May 19, 2004, Juilliard student Sarah Fox was jogging in Inwood Hill Park, New York City. She was wearing earphones. Her battered body was discovered six days after her brutal, life-ending beating in the nearby woods. Fourteen months later, in 2005, another female victim was nearly killed while jogging in the same area. She was attacked at 8:30 a.m. As she was running, her assailant came up on her from behind and grabbed her neck. At the same time, he smeared a substance that reminded her of Vicks VapoRub into her eyes, obscuring her vision.

As she fell to the ground hard, she cut her head. The blood flow from her head wound added to the panic caused by the violent and completely unexpected onslaught. She maintained consciousness, however, and started to scream. Her screaming attracted the attention of a nearby male jogger, who turned around and ran toward her. The perpetrator fled the scene as the male jogger approached. The woman required sixteen stitches, but she lived to tell the tale. She too was wearing earphones.

These types of attacks have been around for as long as head- and earphones. Give yourself a fighting chance. You wouldn't walk through the jungle or the deep woods wearing headphones. Common sense dictates you need to hear in the event a dangerous animal should approach. How long do you think you would stay alive in Alaska's wilderness walking around with headphones? Don't care about the bears? How about the jungles of Southeast Asia, or the deserts of Utah, for that matter? So why in the world, when you are among the most ruthless predators in the world—the human male species— why would you want to deprive yourself of a key defense? Don't wear earphones in public unless you are interested in identifying yourself as a potential target and playing directly into the hands of natural selection.

OPEN YOUR EYES—PUT THE PHONE AWAY

The predator surveyed the crowded bus. He was unsure, but he was desperate for money. After going over the odds in his mind for a couple of minutes, he made his move. He quietly removed the stolen .45 caliber pistol from his pocket and went up to the first victim. He showed the man his firearm and quietly told him to hand over his wallet. The victim, a man who was looking at his phone, was visibly startled to be looking at the barrel of the gun, but he quietly did as he was told. The predator then proceeded with the exact same modus operandi to rob three additional passengers—all of whom were busy with earphones and/or their smartphones so that each one was completely taken by surprise. In fact, the security camera on the bus showed that the preponderance of the passengers were looking at their phones or listening to music with headsets. The fourth victim, also looking at his phone, had a different response. He immediately jumped to his feet and proceeded to hit the predator repeatedly. Only then did other passengers look up from their phones to see that an altercation was taking place. The predator, fortunately for victim number four, was subdued. Interestingly, the man who initially fought back maintained his grip on his phone during the confrontation and could actually be seen putting it away with one hand while engaging the robber with the other. Even when he was fighting for his life, he could not let go of the phone!

Ride any form of public transportation or step into any coffee shop anywhere in the world, and easily 90 percent of the people are engaged with their phones—oblivious to what is happening around them. This phenomenon is so widespread that the internet is replete with humorous video compilations of idiot sticks falling into fountains, off curbs, or walking into doors and poles because their faces and focus were firmly planted on their phones. As a result, the laws of physics take their toll against this rapidly growing subset of the human species like the Grim Reaper collecting hapless souls. Funny to watch but not so much if you are the victim of a violent crime.

"As with earphones, don't focus on your phone in public," I advised my son. "If I told you that field was a potential minefield, you wouldn't walk through it willy-nilly while completely restricting your hearing and your vision, right? So don't do that to yourself in an urban environment." Whereas the chances of your walking through a mine field are low, short of a deployment to a war zone, who among us believes that we could never be a victim of crime?

SIXTH SENSE AND COMMON SENSE

As we walked the streets, we discussed situational awareness and the human mind's incredible ability to talk us out of what we know to be inherently true, to defy common sense, and to ignore our sixth sense. Time and again, survivors of violent crime will state that in hindsight, something seemed wrong. There was an instinctual sense of unease about their attacker (if they had the luxury of seeing him beforehand). Their sixth sense attempted to warn them, but they suppressed their instinct by writing it off with "I didn't want to be rude," or "I told myself I was just imagining things." There is a natural tendency for the untrained mind to attempt to convince itself that "this isn't happening," like the effects of shock on the surprised victim of a stabbing who repeatedly asks, "Why? Why?" as their attacker continues stabbing them with a knife. Or like the victim who believed, even as her attacker pushed her into her apartment, that he must have been skiing because he was wearing a ski mask. So how does this relate to walking down the street?

As my son and I walked, I would point things out. "See that guy standing on the corner over there on our side of the street?" I asked.

"Yeah, what about him?"

"Let's cross over to the other side of the street. I don't like the way he is just standing there," I said, adding, "It's not a reflection on our manhood. We simply saw something that caught our attention, so we will give it a natural and unassuming wide berth.

"Now if we cross and in response he crosses over onto our side, then that constitutes a valuable and visible cue—a warning that there is a potential problem, and we then have time to evaluate courses of action."

And this is the way you should navigate the street. If you see something that gives you pause, avoid it. If you turn your back to retrace your steps, make sure you check behind you. If you observe someone taking an interest in you, and he starts to mirror your movements, consider it a blessing—now you can plan a course of action, whether it's walking into a store, changing your direction, walking to the nearest police station, or preparing to fight for your life.

PARANOIA VERSUS INSTINCTS

There is a clear distinction between being paranoid and listening to your instincts. Being paranoid makes you fearful of everything real and imagined, whereas listening to your instincts and being situationally aware puts your mind on alert when something doesn't feel right. Take driving as an example. When you are on a crowded highway cruising at seventy miles per hour, you are taking in thousands of unconscious signals every second and making split-second decisions to change lanes, accelerate, and slow down based on what your intuition and senses are telling you about the cars around you. When a particular driver's actions—or lack thereof—catch your eye, and you ask, "What the hell is he doing?" your senses ratchet up a notch until you figure it out and take action accordingly. A predator looking for a victim will typically situate himself so he can observe. If you see a person seemingly waiting and looking at people, your instincts should pay additional attention. If that person is occupying a choke point you have to traverse and is dressed in a manner that hides his face, you should enter a higher state of awareness and consider another route. Your instincts are helping you navigate.

Gavin de Becker, in his landmark book *The Gift of Fear* (mandatory reading in my household), describes the case of a mother and her young daughter going to the movie theater with some friends. While waiting in line to get in, a man in line behind them attempted to engage her in conversation. She felt an instinctual dislike of the man but could not really identify the reason. After the movie ended, her friend offered her a ride to her parked car, which was some distance away, but the mother politely turned it down, noting that the weather was nice, and it was just a short walk. Almost instantly, she regretted her decision—again without any discernible reason. As she was walking with her daughter, she noticed to her extreme discomfort that the same man was walking behind them. This correctly set off alarm bells in her mind. Without telling her daughter the reason, she urged her to move more quickly. She started thinking about her actions upon arriving at the car: how she would unlock the car remotely, open the door, and put her daughter in first and then move to her side. As they arrived at the car, she started to execute her plan. However, as she started to get into her side, the man grabbed her from behind. Half in the car and half out, she started kicking at him with all her might. Her heart rate was up, her adrenaline was pumping, and she was engaged in one of nature's most powerful and protective instincts: protecting her child. She had enough presence of mind to realize that her keys were still in her hand and that she could use them to poke his eye with it. And almost without realizing it, she made it happen. As it turned out, she had actually stuck the key in both eyes. She survived the confrontation, and we can draw a multitude of lessons from it.

Firstly, she realized her suppressed instincts were correct. When she realized he was behind her, there was no more attempt to talk herself out of anything. She finally listened to her instincts.

Secondly, she demonstrated that even a modicum of forethought can make a difference. Rather than panic, she thought through what her actions would be: approaching and opening the car. In this case, even a few seconds of forethought made a difference.

Lastly, in her decision to fight, she did not hesitate at the possible moral dilemma many victims encounter in a moment of crisis: the wanton destruction of an assailant's eyes and her decision to mercilessly attack a delicate vulnerability on the body of another human being. She was able to successfully kill her empathy switch when it came to protecting her child. The number of victims who were strangled to death while scratching their attacker's face is beyond count. The real pity is that if they could have reached the face, they could have reached an eye. And if they could have reached the eye, they could have inserted an "intraocular foreign body" (your finger or anything else) into the outer wall of the eye and through the cornea, in which case, everything would have changed in their favor. But that discussion will come later. To her credit, in those moments, the mother fought like a sociopath and won.

She can (and I hope she does) take absolute pride in that victory. She made some mistakes that she will never forget that led to that point of conflict, but when it mattered, she prevailed and won—not to mention the powerful lesson for her daughter. And that has to be a life lesson that made her stronger and more competent. I'm all about avoiding conflict, but if you have to fight for your life or your family, then there are no half measures. Win at all costs and make it easier by learning how.

YOUR CAR

How well do you know your car? For example, I currently have a made-in-the-USA rental car in Saudi Arabia. For reasons that completely escape me, the manufacturer thought having the doors automatically unlock when the car is in park is somehow a good idea. Or alternatively, lock once the car is in motion. It doesn't take much to imagine how a lone woman could become a victim of assault in a car like that. She gets into her car and starts it, and before she can put the car in gear while she is focused on connecting her iPhone to the jack, her assailant gets in through one of the other doors or opens her door. So learn how your car works. Get into the habit of getting in and locking the car door immediately. First things first. After the doors are locked, start it. That way, while you are focused on something else, like plugging your phone into the jack to listen to music or setting your GPS, you can put the car in gear and move quickly if necessary.

Instinct, intuition, common sense, or sixth sense—they've been cultivated and passed down to us through countless generations. It's why our ancestors survived the saber-toothed tigers and why we are walking the planet today so many generations later. When something makes you suspicious or uneasy, listen to it. This is different than outright fear. A child may fear there is a monster under the bed, but just because they believe it doesn't make it so. On the other hand, suspicion is caused by something that makes our level of alert accelerate. It could be caused by a spoken phrase ("Excuse me, do you have the time?"), a person standing nearby, the sound of footsteps coming from behind, or anything else that catches our attention. So when something makes you uneasy, listen. Instinct, coupled with situational awareness appropriate to the situation, becomes a most valuable survival tool.

THINK YOU ARE BEING FOLLOWED?

This happens to women more often than you would think. A 2016 poll conducted by *Runner's World* showed that 43 percent of women respondents indicated they experienced harassment at least sometimes during a run. Thirty percent reported being followed by a man in a car, on a bicycle, or on foot at least once. A woman is minding her own business, and someone takes an interest in her and then starts to follow. This happened to my wife once, when she was pregnant with our daughter, no less. A man attempted to make small talk with her in a store. If my wife has any fault, it's that she is too kind to people, and she politely responded to a question he posed but at the same time did not encourage any further discourse. She felt uncomfortable and noticed that he continued to watch her in the store. A few minutes later when she returned to her car, she noticed the same man was in a car behind her. Married to an operations officer, she has an understanding about the basics of surveillance detection, and we had casually discussed what actions she should take if she ever felt she were being followed. And so she started to drive a route to confirm or deny her suspicions. She deliberately did not return home, as she did not want to reveal to him where she lived—the absolute correct course of action. He made a couple of turns with her, which heightened her concern. After several more turns, however, he was no longer there, and she surmised he broke off from his endeavor, and she cautiously returned home. I praised her for her awareness and her actions. Driving around and making several turns to determine if she were being followed or not was a good idea. The point of making several turns is to make sure the person is not simply going in the same direction. In hindsight, I would have added one component. If she felt that she was being followed, I would have suggested that she drive to the local police station. Had she been on foot, the same principle would apply. Confirm your suspicions and walk to a place where some form of security is present, or make a 911 call and wait in a very public place.

PROJECTING CONFIDENCE

Nature is brutally efficient at weeding out the sick and weak. Part of staying off the menu in an urban environment, where the predators walk on two legs, is appearing confident. I'm not talking about being visibly cocky. That will just draw unwanted attention; rather, you want to project a quiet confidence. Again, I'm not talking about staring down each person you encounter. I'm talking about taking a momentary look at each potential threat. Can you see their hands? Are they focused on you? Do they appear agitated? Are fists clenched? Are their faces covered? Do they look like they belong? Do they appear rational? How are they dressed? A large percentage of criminals wear hoodies, for example. Does that mean that everyone who wears a hoodie is a criminal? Absolutely not. But if you are in an urban environment, and you are about to walk past three adolescents standing around at the entrance to the subway wearing hoodies, should you raise your level of alert? Hell yes. No one gets dressed by accident. Each person chooses the manner in which they present themselves. Many of those who desire to visit violence upon another human being dress in a manner that is conducive to hiding their identities.

What about you? Are you walking with your hands in your pockets? If so, you are slowing your reaction time considerably. Are you projecting a calm confidence? Or do you look scared and hunted? Are you maintaining your situational awareness, or is your face buried in your phone?

When I teach combatives, I show my trainees a video clip that shows a handful of young African American males engaged in the knockout game. In the film clip, captured by two security cameras, you can see a middle-aged white male walking through the five African American youths who were just standing there hanging out. As soon as he walked past them, they all immediately started to follow him. The victim looked behind him and clearly registered that all of the youths were now following him. He then turned his gaze forward again and continued walking. In those intervening seconds before he was brutally attacked, one can only imagine the thoughts running through the victim's mind. Clearly, he was aware of their presence. It was also daylight, and there was traffic on the streets. Chances are he was engaged in what Gavin de Becker would describe as "cross-examining his own feelings." That is to say, he was second-guessing his feelings because even after he turned and looked at them, all following him when they had been standing moments before, he didn't do anything. He may have been thinking, "It's probably nothing," or "If I ignore them it will be OK," or "It's daylight, and there are cars out," or "I'm only imagining it." None of that mattered because one of the youths ran up behind him and hit him with a full, hard swing to the side of his face, knocking him out. We can only speculate on secondary injuries caused from hitting his head against the wall of the building and then the concrete on his way down. The youths just laughed and went about their day, not even bothering to take his backpack or wallet. If you hear running feet, ascertain the cause, and be prepared to fight for your life.

GOT ANY CHANGE, THE TIME, A LIGHT? TIME TO RAMP UP YOUR SENSES

Predators will very frequently close the distance by distracting you verbally in order to get close. If anyone attempts to engage you on the street, you should enter into a state of high alert—they want something, and it's rarely the thing they are asking about. Raising one or both hands while responding will place you in a better position to react physically should the need arise. Don't just ignore and put them out of your mind. Maintain your situational awareness of their movements after the exchange. If necessary, change your course to a more well-lit area or into a store. The point is not to ignore and forget, or you do so at your peril.

CULTIVATE YOUR INTENT

In that moment of truth, as you cycle through the denial-deliberation-and-action cycle, you want to get to the action as quickly as possible. That action response must be as violent and effective as possible. The first time you think about it should not be when it is happening. Learn how to fight (more later) and visualize how you would achieve visiting violence upon another human being. Practice. Your desired end state is to fight like a sociopath to defeat a sociopath—and then rejoin society.

Sometime after our urban jaunt, my son told me that he appreciated that walk and that he took away some valuable lessons from it. I hope those lessons will last a lifetime.

KEY CONCEPTS

- Don't deprive yourself of key senses. Ditch the earphones and stay off your phone in public.

- Predators are looking for the weak and the unaware. As you navigate the urban landscape, avoid anything, or anyone, who causes you pause. There is no slight to your honor by crossing the street or reversing course to avoid a potential problem. If that problem crosses the street with you, then you have time to make decisions before things escalate.

- Looks matter. Project a quiet confidence. Learn to look for clues: body language and dress that could suggest a potential problem.

- Dress appropriately so as not to stand out. This is true for both a crime and counterterrorism context. The Bali bombers were hunting Americans for their attack. Of the 202 deaths, seven were U.S. citizens. Most of the others were Australian. The Jemaah Islamiyah bombers looked for venues that had a lot of Westerners—easily identified by their style of dress.

- Understand how your car works. As soon as you get in, lock it. Then start your car. After that, set up your music, GPS, or whatever, and be on your way.

- Be wary of anyone who attempts to engage you in conversation.

- Develop a mindset that while you are a sane and law-abiding citizen, there may come a time when you will have to fight like a sociopath to defeat a sociopath. This does not make you a criminal or less humane. You are cultivating the ability to defend yourself effectively and only when necessary. Accept that this will be an ongoing process. Visualize it and mentally prepare for it.

8

DEFENDING
YOUR HOME

PRACTICAL MEASURES

"I've got help on the way. Stay on the line."

"She has a hammer here."

"Don't touch it. Don't touch it. Just leave it there."

"She hit him in the head several times. That's the hammer he had with him. She struck him, and she strangled him, and she thinks he's dead."

— 911 CALL ON SEPTEMBER 6, 2006

On the evening of Wednesday, September 6, 2006, fifty-one-year-old emergency room nurse Susan Kuhnhausen ended her shift at Providence Portland Medical Center. After stopping at the salon on the way home, she arrived at her house to find a note from her husband of eighteen years:

"Sue, haven't been sleeping. Had to get away—Went to the beach...Luv ME."

She perused her mail in the driveway, then went inside and took off her shoes. She suddenly noticed that the first-floor bedroom seemed darker and wondered if she had forgotten to open the curtains.

It was at that moment that her assailant emerged from behind her bedroom door with rubber gloves and a claw hammer in his hand.

The brain can only go where the brain has gone before.

Susan instantly understood that she was in the realm of asocial violence. A highly experienced emergency room nurse, she had faced her share of life-and-death situations with wild, drugged, and unruly patients. She knew that to lessen the blow from the hammer she needed to close the distance. (Had she turned and fled, she would have surely been run down and beaten to death.) Her assailant still managed to land a glancing blow on the side of her head. While five inches shorter than her assailant, she did outweigh him, and in the ensuing moments, she experienced a surge of adrenaline and entered into the fight of her life.

During the struggle, she managed to gain possession of the hammer, and now she swung it, striking his moving head with partial blows three, possibly four, times. In spite of this (he too was in the fight of his life), he was able to regain control of the hammer, but she grabbed his throat with all of her strength. As his face literally started to change color, she let go of his throat and attempted to run. Her assailant, later identified as Edward

Haffrey, caught up with her in the hallway and punched her twice, dropping her to the floor. As he stood over her with the hammer in his hand, she told herself that she needed to get the hammer.

She couldn't recall exactly how she did it, but somehow, she was able to upset his balance so that he fell to the floor. And then she started to bite him. On his arm, leg, thigh—even through his zipper and into his genitals.

Fighting on the floor in the hallway, she crawled on top of him and started to choke him until he finally stopped moving. Grabbing the hammer, she ran to her neighbor's house, and they called 911. The encounter was estimated to have lasted an incredible fourteen minutes.

It turned out that her husband Mike had hired Edward Dalton Haffey, an ex-con, to kill Susan. She became a statistic in a group that you never want to join: she was one of the 58 percent of women who become potential or actual murder victims by an intimate partner.

The brain can only go where the brain has gone before. Susan did an incredible job. She had experience in violence through decades of work in a hospital emergency room, and she had received some defense training. In her moment of truth, her brain started going through its list of experiences. She had the presence of mind to close the gap and fought with everything she had. When it mattered, she fought like a sociopath; she became a wolf to devour a wolf, and she lived to tell the tale.

According to the Department of Justice, between 2005 and 2007, about 3.7 million burglaries occurred each of those years.

Household members were present in about one-third of the cases and slightly more than one out of four became victims of violent crime. "Simple assault" was the most common form of violence. (IMHO "simple" has different meanings for different people. A Brazilian jujitsu practitioner and a grandmother might both be victims of "simple" assault, although I would hazard a guess that the outcome for the victim could be vastly different.) Offenders were known to their victims about 65 percent of the time. About 12 percent of victims encountered an intruder armed with a gun. For the asocial predator intent on crime beyond a burglary, a home offers privacy.

So you can play the odds and hope that nothing ever happens (sheep), or you can take active measures to prepare for an event and increase the odds that you and your family will come out unscathed—hopefully with nothing more than a few insurance bills (sheepdog/sheepdog-like).

PRACTICAL MEASURES IN HOME PROTECTION

There are a few measures that you can take today that will make your home protection challenges easier:

- **A camera system for the house perimeter.** There are a multitude of choices in this realm. Many are internet-based and allow you to watch from wherever you are (as in my case when I was in Afghanistan and could see intruders in Virginia). They are affordable and worth every penny. A service like Ring also informs you about crimes in your town, and you can distribute Ring images to all Ring owners if you need to spread the word about possible criminal activity. You can extend your camera network to the inside as well. (Imagine being able to watch an intruder downstairs when you are upstairs.) When you set up your cameras, think like a criminal. Where would he likely try to break in? The window in the back of the house, for example. Those are the locations where you want to place your cameras. You can create a "defense in-depth" concept by having a couple of indoor cameras to detect and video any intruder who gets inside.

· **A camera with a doorbell feature.** There are too many reported instances of a predator gaining entry to a home while posing as a repairman or some other contrived (and in some cases real) guise. Practically speaking, never open the door if you can avoid it. You can address the person (and see them) though one of the many commercially available doorbell cameras. Ring and Arlo are both popular brands. Often, a burglar will knock on the front door to case the residence. If no one answers, he will usually proceed to the back to execute his break-in. If you are a woman and open the door in response, you are placing yourself at an unnecessary risk. Assaults have happened when the criminal asked to speak to "the man of the house" to ascertain who else might be home. A predator needs privacy, and if you open the door, you are at risk of providing that privacy in your most secure sanctuary. Cameras in each location will give you time to prepare accordingly.

· **Sensors for windows and doors.** Had any of the three idiot sticks prowling outside my home cracked a seal on a door or window, an alarm would have sounded. Any intruder who remains in the house after such an event likely has murderous intent and is an excellent candidate for deadly force. You can place the sensors on every door and window and arm them through the service when you go to bed or are out of the house. Like camera services, these alarm services charge a reasonable monthly fee. In the event of an alarm, the company will call to ensure it was not a mistake and will notify authorities if necessary. Sensors typically cost about thirty-five dollars each. A less expensive alternative to secure your window would be to drill holes and emplace pins to prevent anyone from opening the window from the outside. (Latches are easily defeated by a skilled home invader.) Now, if you feel compelled to advertise that you have an alarm system, I would recommend that you not put stickers on your windows and signs on your front lawn with the name of the actual system you have. If you advertise what your defense is, you are giving the criminal good intelligence. Better if the surprise is on him.

- **Motion-detection lights.** When I was in Afghanistan, I did not have motion-detection lights on the outside perimeter of my home. I had them installed by a reputable electrician after the incident, and I am convinced that had they been in place to begin with, the intruders would never have walked up to my garage and rear deck and tested my doors and windows. These lights can be pricey but are an excellent means of perimeter defense. When the light turns on, the intruder has no way of knowing if the owner turned them on or motion turned them on. Any intruder who continues anyway likely has murderous intent and is definitely a candidate for deadly force. Something like the RAB 360 works quite well and is a favored brand by many electricians for their reliability and longevity.
- **Dogs.** Dogs often (but not always) are the first to hear something amiss in the home. I can't count the number of near heart attacks or startle responses my German shepherd has triggered in me through vigorous barking when someone walked up to the door before they knocked or rang the doorbell. Lapdog or guard dog, these lovable crea-

tures can eliminate or denigrate any unhappy surprises. They need and deserve love and discipline (read *How to be Your Dog's Best Friend* by the monks of New Skete), but they are wonderful companions and effective deterrents.

- **Firearms.** Firearms are not for everyone. If you are going to have one (or more) in your home, then you need to shoot them frequently so that you have the fundamentals of marksmanship and range safety ingrained into your psyche. Also, be familiar with the laws of your city and state.

- **Placement of car keys in the bedroom.** Most people leave their car keys in an easy-to-locate place in their kitchen. Thieves of course know this, and it is not uncommon to have your house broken into and your car stolen to add insult to injury. But consider keeping your car keys in your bedroom. In the event of a break-in while you are home, you can activate the car alarm from a distance to distract the thieves and hopefully cut short their activities.

- **Drill.** Think of potential home intrusion and natural disaster scenarios and the actions you and each family member would take. Walk through it from time to time with family members to refresh the training. And remember that in crisis, you will default to your lowest level of training.

FIREARMS IN THE HOME

The sound of a shotgun chambering a round is universally recognized throughout the world. There is nothing like it. If someone is walking down your hallway and they hear that sound—and keep coming—then you know without doubt, you are about to have a deadly force encounter. I keep a twelve-gauge shotgun for home defense. It is an awesome close-quarter weapon, and the shot (unless it's a slug) won't typically go through the wall to inadvertently shoot your neighbor or other household members. Also, with the nature of buckshot (many small pellets spreading out as they gain distance after the shot), you don't have to worry about aiming. Just point and shoot.

As with any firearm, routine practice is vital so that when under stress, you can load it and operate it safely without thinking. For example, ensuring a straight trigger finger until you have an identified target is a critical component to handling a firearm. If you have your finger on the trigger and you undergo a startle response, what do you imagine will happen? Knowing how to ensure you see what is in front of, behind, and around your target before firing is also important. This is hard to do when your heart is pounding and adrenaline is coursing throughout your body. Or knowing how not to flag (inadvertently pointing your weapon) at any of your family members while moving with the firearm. If you live in an apartment or even a single-family home, what will happen if you miss and the round goes through a wall? Frequent practice will ensure you know how to check to see if the weapon is loaded properly.

Another consideration is where to store it along with its ammo. It doesn't take a criminal genius to figure out that most homeowners hide their weapons within easy reach of their beds, which for most people means under/behind the bed or in the bedroom closet. The obvious danger to this is that you come home some day and interrupt a robbery in progress, and the robber has found your weapon. The odds of that scenario ending well are greatly diminished. For this reason, I highly recommend a furniture concealment device where you can hide the weapon but still easily access it in a time of need. There are a growing number of commercial options available.

For example, I have weapons hidden in furniture concealment devices. All I have to do is take them out and they're already locked and loaded and ready to go. I also have handguns in concealment devices that one of my kids could conceivably find by accident, and that weapon requires that the slide be racked (pulled back and released to chamber a round) one time to avoid an accidental discharge by small hands. That is a temporary solution, as they will grow stronger with age. The last part of that is teaching children what and what not to do around firearms. After all, kids do everything they are supposed to do all the time, right?

Are you mentally prepared for the loud sound of shooting a firearm inside your house without ear protection? Are you mentally prepared for the possibility of the opposite taking place and experiencing auditory exclusion where you are so focused on the threat that you don't hear the firearm at all?

Most importantly, are you prepared to take a human life? Because if you are unsure about that point, you most definitely should not possess a firearm. As with most concepts presented in this book, mental preparation is a key facet to dealing with stressful situations.

You also need to understand the gun laws for your particular state, as they can vary drastically. For example, Florida and Texas have pretty clear-cut "stand your ground" laws, which basically mean that if you feel threatened, you can justify use of lethal force. Whereas in Virginia, there is no such legal concept, nor is there a castle doctrine for protecting your home. If my wife had shot one of the intruders while they were on the deck or even inside the house on the ground floor, she could have found herself in legal jeopardy. But if the intruder had gone upstairs and ignored her warnings for him to leave, she would have been justified to use lethal force. I've often said I would rather be judged by twelve than carried by six, but you should understand—at least in broad terms—the consequences of your actions.

If you own a firearm or carry one, consider joining an insurance/legal protective group like U.S. LawShield or the United States Concealed Carry Association, and enroll in NRA online training, such as "Refuse to Be a Victim." However you may feel about the NRA's political lobbying efforts, they still excel at teaching firearms and personal safety.

YOUR CAR AND GPS

GPS devices are rapidly being replaced by smartphones. If you do keep a GPS in your car, however, avoid having anything marked "Home" stored in it. You don't want a car thief or valet looking up your home address while they steal your car or park it. If you need to have a GPS marker for home, pick a nearby landmark and refer to it instead (on the assumption that if you can find it, you can find your way home from there without the GPS).

SHADES OF GRAY: PLANS RARELY SURVIVE FIRST CONTACT, ESPECIALLY POOR PLANS

You are in a deep sleep when, suddenly, your alarm is triggered, making you sit bolt upright in bed. I think you would agree that *now* is not the time to think about what you should do. If so, what should you do? In typical CIA instructor fashion, I will answer that "it depends." (That answer always has and always will frustrate generations of CIA trainees.) But it actually does depend on a number of factors. Mainly, do you have a plan in place? And how complete is it? Poor planning is almost as bad as no planning. So let's look at some variations of the same scenario. See if you can identify potential problems and gauge how your own plan stands up. In this manner, you can start your own planning or adjust your own defensive posture to bring it closer to maximum effectiveness.

NIGHT SCENARIO 1

Susan woke suddenly with a crushing weight on top of her. In her startle response, she tried to scream, but a hand was covering her mouth. To her horror, she realized there was a man on top of her wearing a mask. He had something in his hand and was pressing it against her neck and was saying something—warning her to stay still and remain quiet. Why didn't the alarm sound? She couldn't remember if she had turned it on. She had forgotten in the past.

Lessons Learned

- Obviously, there are any number of variations on this first scenario. But in this case, it's clear that the victim did not make her home protection measures a force of habit; rather, she left her fate to the gods.
- Clearly, scenario 1 is a nightmare scenario. She took minimal precautions, and while she had an alarm system in place, she was lax in setting it.
- Perhaps she knows some combatives and knows to bide her time and strike the eyes, throat, and groin in order to debilitate her attacker. This, of course, would require practice and forethought.

NIGHT SCENARIO 2

Susan froze—ears straining—as she tried to convince herself it was not happening. It must be a mistake. The noise from the alarm set every fiber of her being on edge. But she tried to rationalize it as something else. There must be something wrong with the alarm. Her chest was pounding from the sudden increase in her heart rate, and she found it increasingly hard to think. Call 911? Where was the firearm? She couldn't remember if it was loaded. Was it? With sudden doubt, she wondered if she should try to find some other kind of weapon. Should she stay there or go down and check out the house? She was starting to panic.

Lessons Learned

- We can see that she was exhibiting the very human trait of trying to talk herself out of what she knows to be true. The "this can't be happening" mindset is an attempt to cope with the stress of the moment, but it's a fatal mindset.
- She hasn't thought about recognizing the effects of fear— the rapid rise in heart rate or how to bring it under control. Once your heart rate hits about 240 bpm, the animal brain takes over and blind panic sets in.
- Like many people, she may have a firearm, but it appears that she rarely—if ever—practices with it. She is so unsure that she is already thinking of alternative weapons.
- And now she has a nagging curiosity to go downstairs and find out the cause of the alarm, hoping it's just a mistake with one of the sensors. Not a good move, as she could be surprised by the intruder or run into a responding police officer who may just see a person with a weapon. Either way, not cool...

NIGHT SCENARIO 3

Susan awoke from a dead sleep as she tried to comprehend the sound that woke her and realized the alarm was on. Her heart rate immediately increased, and a dozen thoughts entered her mind simultaneously. She hurried to her furniture concealment device and took out a Glock pistol. She couldn't remember: Was it ready to fire? Or did she place it in home-storage mode? Quickly, she crossed the room and locked the door. The phone rang as the security monitoring service called to check on the cause of the alarm. She told them she needed help. She stood breathlessly in front of the bedroom door, holding her firearm, her heart pounding. She forgot to check if there was a round in the chamber. She meant to go to the range more often. "The police will be here soon," she thought to herself.

Lessons Learned

- This Susan was better prepared. Although she did not practice with her firearm enough to know if it was loaded with a round in the chamber or if it was in home-storage mode, she could have done a press check (partially pulling back the slide to ensure a round was in the chamber) or simply racked the slide (pulling the slide all the way back and releasing to chamber a round) one time. Consequently, she was unsure what state her firearm was in: if the door to her bedroom opened and she identified a threat and pulled the trigger, would the gun discharge? Not knowing whether a gun is loaded is the number one cause of accidental discharges (and an example of natural selection in action).

Susan awoke from a dead sleep to the unmistakable sound of the alarm. She knew this because she set the alarm before bed just as she did every night. As her heartbeat continued to accelerate, she remembered to take a three-count breath in, hold it for a couple of seconds and take a three-count breath out, and almost immediately, she felt her heart rate starting to stabilize. She repeated this process several times and felt her heart rate and breathing returning to a more manageable level—she was consciously controlling her fear with the breathing exercise. Meanwhile, she was reaching for her handgun in her concealment device. She knew it was ready to shoot because she always stored it that way, and she did a press check before putting it away after the range last week. With weapon in hand, she moved to a spot in her room that offered some concealment and allowed her to shoot anyone in the doorway. She knew the door was locked with the deadbolt because she locked it routinely every night. The phone rang, and it was the security company. She told them she needed help, and they promised to call the police. As she covered the door, she maintained a straight trigger finger (which she will do until she has identified a target), and the muzzle was pointed slightly down. She put the phone on speaker and dialed 911—not wanting to put all of her trust into the security company—and told 911 there was a "home invasion in progress" (guaranteed to get a rapid police response). She started to scan the security cameras from her phone as she waited. On high alert, she was ready for whatever might come through the door.

Lessons Learned

- The Susan in scenario 4 did much better. Clearly, she

ingrained the habit to use her alarm. She took the time to make it a part of her routine.

- She also recognized immediately the physical effects of fear (rapid heart rate) and how to mitigate it through breathing exercises.
- She had a concealment device for her firearm, and she always put it in the device loaded and ready to fight should she need it in an emergency. She always double-checked that there was a round in the chamber with a press check before putting the firearm into the cavity of the concealment device.
- She moved to a predetermined point in her room to cover the door (best not to be standing immediately in front of the door if you don't know what is on the other side).
- She also had a deadbolt on her bedroom door—it is not kick proof, but it will definitely buy time. She responded to the security company call and correctly called 911, not wanting to rely solely on the security company.
- She scanned her cameras with her smartphone to see what was happening in the house.

NIGHT SCENARIO 5

The motion alert on Susan's smartphone woke her up. She could see from the glare of the lights outside that the motion-detection lights had turned on in the backyard. The alarm remained silent, and she knew that she set it before bed, as always. She checked the outdoor cameras and saw that she had a couple of additional camera notifications on her phone. When she checked, she could see a person wearing a hoodie and gloves had entered the range of the light and ran away when the light turned on. Just to be sure, she retrieved her firearm from the concealment device. She always stored her weapon in a ready-to-fire mode and did not have to think about it when she retrieved it. She called 911 and reported a home intrusion in progress. She checked each of her cameras and saved the video clip of the would-be intruder while she waited for the police to arrive. She did not put the weapon away until she had eyes on the police officer outside the front door, and she informed the officer she was putting her weapon away before opening the door. She promptly showed him the video.

Lessons Learned

- This Susan clearly had a happy ending to what otherwise might have been a traumatic, possibly life-altering experience.
- She had installed motion detection lights. If a criminal insists on breaking in after the lights go on and then triggers a door/window sensor and still comes in despite the alarm, you can be sure you have a deadly force encounter on your hands. Be prepared to fight for your life.
- She kept the video clips to pass to the police as evidence. With some systems, like Ring, you could share the video clips with neighborhood Ring owners.
- She kept her firearm in a concealment device and had it ready to deploy and knew the status of her firearm. Familiarity breeds competence, and it's clear she routinely spent time on a range and practiced dry firing techniques at home (practicing the sequence of shooting without any bullets in the weapon).
- She had cameras on her perimeter and main doors, but she also had a couple inside to monitor any unwanted activity there.

DAYTIME BREAK-INS

When we think about home invasions, we generally think about nighttime break-ins. Certainly, that is what my family experienced. But about 6 percent more break-ins take place between 6 a.m. and 6 p.m. While that is not a huge difference, the point is that just over half of home break-ins take place during the day and usually when the occupants are not home. Typically, a robber will knock or ring the bell at the front and, if there is no answer, make their way to the rear of the house, where there is more privacy to facilitate their break-in. Let's look at a range of possibilities and various levels of awareness and preparation.

DAY SCENARIO 1

Susan heard the doorbell ring. She looked through the peephole, half thinking it was a reminder why she wanted to get a doorbell camera. The man was wearing some kind of utility uniform, so even though she wasn't expecting anyone, she opened the door.

"Good morning," he stated. "I'm with County Water, and I understand there is a problem with your main valve?"

Susan had no idea what he was referring to.

"No problem," he explained, "it only takes a minute, and according to our records, you may have a slow leak. I can check it real quick just to make sure. Usually, the main valve is in the kitchen."

Susan instinctually didn't feel comfortable for reasons she could not clearly identify. But he seemed official, so she waved him in. Her battered body was found a day later when a concerned friend called police because Susan was not responding to calls or her door.

Lessons Learned

- Even though she had a peephole, she still opened the door. Once the door was opened, the attacker only had to determine if she was alone. He manipulated his way into the house, and the sanctuary was turned into a tomb.
- The uniform colored her perception of the danger.
- She did not listen to her intuition that something was wrong. People under duress generally go through three emotions: disbelief, deliberation, and action. This cycle can last fractions of seconds to hours (think of some of the victims of 9/11 who remained in the towers for hours after the planes crashed into them). Some never get past disbelief and deliberation.

DAY SCENARIO 2

Susan heard the doorbell. She looked on her smartphone at her Ring app and saw a man in a uniform at the door. Turning on the speaker from her phone, she asked if she could help him. The man explained he was from the water company, and they had a report of a slow leak in her main valve. Susan—who was alone—indicated she was not aware of the leak or a visit. The man offered to check it quickly, noting the valve was likely in the kitchen, and it would only take a minute. Susan politely indicated her boyfriend/husband/father/friend (pick one) was busy at the moment, but that he would check it and get back to the company. The man seemed uncomfortable with this and stated he would be back another time and left.

Lessons Learned

- Susan did not open the door. Even though she was healthy and studied mixed martial arts, she correctly assessed there was no need to open the door and managed the entire conversation through the speaker of her Ring Doorbell—and captured it all on video to boot. Perfect.
- Susan did not fall for the "it only takes a minute" and indicated she was not alone (even though she was).
- Even if it was a legitimate call from the water company, the company did not warn the homeowner. Susan can now check with the company to see if the visit was legitimate or not and reschedule another appointment on the off chance it was legit. And if was not legit, she has the photo and video evidence to give to the police.

DAY SCENARIO 3

Susan was at work when she noticed a motion detect on her smartphone, indicating something was moving in range of the camera. Thinking it was probably a deer or neighborhood cat, she was surprised to see a man at her front door. A minute later, the same man was at her back door, and she could see him testing the windows. He then took something out of his pocket and hit the window in the door, reached in, and unlocked the door. But the minute he opened the door, the door sensor alarm went off. The man froze at the sound and then quickly ran off. A moment later Susan received a call from the alarm monitoring company, and she explained that she was at work but that she had witnessed a man breaking the window on her back door. The alarm company said they would call the police, and she decided to do the same. She starting preparing the video and still shots she would give the police as evidence.

Lessons Learned

- This worked out exactly the way it should have for Susan. The video and the sensors did their jobs, as did the monitoring service. But not leaving anything to chance, she called the police herself anyway. And now the police have evidence and an identifiable suspect.

- Susan should wait for the police to arrive at her house before she goes in as a precaution.

KEY CONCEPTS

- Motion-detection lights are an excellent deterrent. Hire an electrician to put them up. Place them in obvious places, like your front and back doors, and garage doors. Also, think like a criminal. Put them in a place where a criminal would want to access your home in privacy (like in the backyard outside of the dining room window, for example). Intruders don't know if someone inside turned on the lights or if they are motion activated. Few will stay to find out. This is not the place to save pennies; go with the best option a reputable electrician recommends. It will be money well spent.

- Security camera systems and door/window sensors are competitively priced and effective.

- Put up a video doorbell that you can answer from anywhere with your smartphone. Never open the door if you do not absolutely have to; otherwise, you risk having your sanctuary becoming your tomb.

- Dogs and guns are excellent home defense assets but require a higher level of care and practice.

- If you keep firearms in the house, know how to use them through regular live-fire training, and know the laws of your state regarding "stand your ground" and "castle doctrine."

- Consider how you will store your firearms. There are some excellent commercial concealment devices and quick access safes available on the market that will allow you to store your weapons loaded and ready to go.
- Practice. Practice. Practice. The brain can only go where the brain has been before. This means you should think of various scenarios and work out how you would handle them. Drill for those scenarios when possible, using the principles of slow practice. Visualizing each step of the scenario is an excellent means of preparing mentally.
- If you have children at home, teach them not to touch firearms (especially if they go to someone's home or if other children come to your home). If they find a firearm, they should inform an adult.
- Consider joining something like U.S. LawShield or United States Concealed Carry Association if you have a firearm in the home or you conceal-carry, as they offer legal benefits specifically for gun owners. Enroll in online training to enhance your knowledge and skills.

9

FIREARMS

MASS SHOOTINGS, CONCEALED CARRY CONSIDERATIONS, AND THE HEEL OF ACHILLES

I don't believe in revolvers at all. A lot of these fanatics who mean business would take all five or six charges and yet get home with their knives though they probably would die directly afterwards.

—MAJOR B. A. COOMBE, DEPUTY ASSISTANT
QUARTER MASTER, KABUL FIELD FORCE,
BRITISH ARMY, AFGHANISTAN, 1880

SCHOOL AND MASS SHOOTINGS—A MODERN AMERICAN PHENOMENA

I am a gun owner and a lifelong shooting enthusiast. I own four pistols and a shotgun and have a concealed carry permit (and frequently carry a concealed handgun in public). I firmly believe in a citizen's right to self-defense and in the right to defend their home. But at the same time, it distresses me that it is appallingly easy to obtain a concealed carry permit, and due to poor central oversight in the sales system, it is too easy to obtain a weapon. The result? Our society is literally and figuratively awash in firearms. It's crept up on us over the past fifty years, and now we are collectively feeling the consequences.

For those who grew up in the 1960s and 1970s, except for certain collectors, no one had assault-type rifles, and in rural areas, teenagers routinely brought their hunting rifles to school during hunting season so they could hit the woods after. In the 1960s and 1970s, if you went into a gun store, the preponderance of guns were handguns and hunting rifles. But now, when you walk into a gun store, military-type assault weapons account for the vast majority of long gun sales. They are now the rule rather than the exception.

The NRA has always been the flagship for hunting safety and firearms training. And while it still excels in those mandates, a part of the NRA has waded too deeply into the morass of politics, weighing in and swaying elections based only on the candidates' stances on weapons. That the NRA could defend "bump stocks" (a modification that allows the shooter to mimic a machine-gun-like rate of fire) after the Nevada shootings is stunning, considering that in the span of eleven minutes, the gunman fired over 1,000 rounds, killed fifty-eight people, and wounded up to 800 (either directly or indirectly as a result of the stampede that occurred).

I'm a member of the NRA and a certified instructor for the Refuse To Be a Victim block of instruction. The NRA does a lot of good, both in education and in protecting Second Amendment rights. At the same time, I find it hard to imagine that the NRA of the early 1970s would have defended the bump stock as a Constitutional right. In the first four months of 2019, the United States experienced 150 mass shootings (a gun attack in which at least four people were killed or injured), according to the Gun Violence Archive. None of these shootings were committed by good, firearm-owning citizens; rather, it was the proliferation of weapons in society that allowed people with evil intent to succeed in carrying out these violent acts. School shootings and active shooter incidents are now so frequent in our society that we are numb to it.

ANNUAL GUN DEATHS SOMETIMES EXCEED COMBAT DEATHS FOR AN ENTIRE CONFLICT

In 2017, the U.S. experienced almost 40,000 deaths by gunshot. About 60 percent were suicides and 37 percent were homicides, according to the *New York Times*. (This leads me to speculate that the remaining 3 percent must have been natural selection in action—accidents by idiot sticks.) This type of violence is virtually unheard of in many parts of the world where I have lived and worked. When you are living in the U.S., those statistics are somehow easy to brush off or ignore. But when I was living overseas, looking from the outside in, the impact of those statistics can be quite alarming. Or if we look at it another way:

- The 40,000 gun deaths in 2017 is 7,000 less than all U.S. combat deaths from the entire Vietnam War from 1962 to 1972.
- The 40,000 gun deaths in 2017 is *ten* times the number of all combat deaths in Iraq between 2003 and March 2019.
- The 40,000 gun deaths in 2017 is more than *twenty* times the combat deaths in Afghanistan between October 2001 and May 2019.
- If we average 40,000 deaths a year as in 2017, then it would take between seven and eight years to reach the total number of U.S. combat deaths of World War II (roughly the period from 2012 to 2019).

Just about anyone on any side of the gun issue can come up with supporting data to bolster their beliefs, and I have no doubt alienated friends on both sides of the debate. Figures vary, but undoubtedly, legal firearms owners have used their firearms in a defensive capacity several hundred thousand times a year. And in the current political climate, there is fear in the gun community that political candidates are moving to ban guns entirely (not a move I support). But what is crystal clear is that this argument is endless. Moreover, much of the debate is moot, as now, more than any time in our history, more weapons are in circulation in society. And the types of weapons available to the general public are more lethal than at any point in the past. We are way past the point where simply outlawing weapons is the solution, as there are simply too many in circulation to make that feasible. Perversely, the fact that there are so many weapons in our society is the precise reason why responsible gun owners should carry. While initially opposed to the idea that teachers should be armed, I would actually support that course of action if the teacher met certain proficiency standards and had holsters with some kind of retention mechanism to prevent anyone from simply grabbing their firearm. If school shooters thought that the chance of meeting a swift death at the hands of an armed defender was extremely high, there would be a lot fewer school shootings (and a lot fewer thoughts and prayers going around, which as far as I can tell, have achieved absolutely nothing).

ACTIONS AGAINST AN ACTIVE SHOOTER

So what do we tell our children about how to handle school shootings? You can rely on the school and hope that turning off the light and staying quiet works. For younger children, we may have little choice. Getting out of a window and running to safety may be the best viable course of action. But older children and adults—those who can physically affect an outcome—do have better choices. What happens when the shooter enters the room? This is no easy answer, but when faced with that choice, the only answer is to attack and shut off the brain of the attacker, as there is nothing more dangerous than the human mind. A weapon is only a danger if it is in the hands of a person who can consciously wield it.

A school shooter is looking for easy targets, and he does not expect resistance—precisely the two reasons why he chose the school as a target in the first place. Hiding under the table at that point for an older child is an invitation to die. Attacking gives you a choice. Knowing where and how to strike to shut off another human's ability to think is also key. Once the brain is shut off through death or unconsciousness, the threat is over. Several students rushing the shooter and striking him in the throat/eyes/testicles stands a greater chance of success than simply hoping he will go away or not notice you.

Where to hit? Go for the neck. A forearm strike to the neck with as much force as you can muster will work wonderfully if you connect. A violent hit to the throat or the back of the neck can result in a lethal blow. A strike to either side of the neck can effectively cause a knockout, as it interrupts the blood flow to the brain. The eyes. Any foreign object entering a shooter's eye will suddenly change the odds in your favor as you deliver a follow-up injury. A solid hit to the groin will achieve the same. Targeting counts. Injury Dynamics and Target Focus Training are two combative systems that give these blows great focus, and we will cover these strikes later.

BEWARE OF THE MOB MENTALITY

In a mass shooting incident, just because everyone is running out into the hallways because the fire alarm is on doesn't mean you should too. If you hear anything remotely similar to a gunshot or firecrackers—and then the fire alarm goes off—don't automatically start to evacuate because it could be a ploy by the shooter to get people into the hallway. Stop, think, assess, decide, and then act—or in Air Force fighter pilot vernacular, execute the OODA loop: observe, orient, decide, act. In this day and age, and as in every other scenario we have looked at, you need to think about how you will react in advance. Don't wait until the moment arrives to decide. And this means actively teaching our children to hone their judgement (no easy task).

FIREARMS AND CONCEALED CARRY

For better or for worse, the option of obtaining a concealed carry permit is quite easy in many states. I personally carry a concealed handgun the majority of time I am out and about. This is a conscious decision, likely born from spending over two years of my professional life in Afghanistan and many years of other assignments in which firearms were authorized for self-protection. Personally, I like the feeling of having a deadly force option—beyond hands and improvised weapons—if necessary to protect myself or my family. If you are going to carry a firearm, however, there are a few considerations.

If you aren't willing to take a life and face the legal and moral consequences—and everything that entails—don't carry one. You are more of a danger to yourself. If you brandish a firearm without intent to use it, there is a strong likelihood you will be shot with your own weapon.

If you are going to carry, it is absolutely essential to keep your skills up. Or if you don't shoot now, receive quality instruction and make a concerted effort to maintain the skill. This means dry fire practice (practicing the firing sequence without ammo) and range time so that you can draw your weapon, acquire a target, control your trigger squeeze, and actually hit what you are aiming at. To really become proficient, you will want to practice in different light levels, around various obstacles, shooting from cars, noise, shooting while moving, after running or exercising to get your heart rate up, and so on. It also means understanding trigger control and how to keep a straight trigger finger until your front site is on an identified target—and you know what is around and behind that target.

If you are going to carry, consider the impact on your children. They will see it. They will likely discover where you store it. Make sure it is secure from them. Make sure they learn from an early age to not touch a firearm and to inform an adult should they find one. This latter point is particularly important if they are at a friend's house.

If you have a child who has behavioral issues, don't make the mistake of teaching him or her how to shoot. Ask Nancy Lanza, mother of Sandy Hook school shooter Adam Lanza. On December 14, 2012, Adam shot her to death in her home and then went to Sandy Hook Elementary School and shot to death twenty first graders and six adults. According to FBI documents, he was "singularly focused and obsessed with mass murders and spree killings" and looked upon school shooters "with respect and understanding." According to one person who knew Adam Lanza from online discussions, he "devoted almost all of his internet activity to researching and discussing mass killings." Two of his online personas went by the names of German and Canadian school shooters Tim Kret-schmer and Kimveer Gill. Nancy Lanza decided that teaching Adam how to shoot was somehow a good idea. According to his father, neither he nor his ex-wife ever suspected Adam was dangerous.

Ask yourself, if you have a firearm, are you more likely to get into a violent social encounter with someone that you otherwise would not? This is an important consideration. Just look at the high number of road rage incidents and arguments over petty issues that erupt—and are more likely to erupt—if you feel invincible. Chances are, you can think of someone you know who you feel is too emotionally immature to walk around with a weapon but does so anyway. If you take an honest look at yourself or find yourself taking risks you wouldn't normally take because now you are armed, better to leave the firearm at home.

So assuming you are dedicated to learning and practicing, and have come to grips with the potential legal and moral consequences of having a firearm in the home—and as they relate to children—which firearm and how best to carry?

SEMIAUTOMATIC VERSUS REVOLVER

A semiautomatic handgun allows you to send a bullet downrange with each successive trigger squeeze. The energy from the fired cartridge loads the next bullet into the chamber. A semiautomatic can hold more rounds (eight to nineteen, depending on the weapon) than a revolver, and it takes less pressure to pull the trigger, which enhances accuracy. Go to any gun store and you will find that the semiautomatic reigns supreme in shooting circles. Thirty years ago, revolvers were the firearm of choice. A revolver is generally a five- or six-shot weapon and relies on the mechanical turning of the cylinder to fire the next round. Trigger pull generally requires more effort than a semiautomatic (unless the hammer is cocked beforehand). And because of that, there is less chance of an accidental discharge with a revolver, rendering them safer than the semiautomatic. Semiautomatics, on the other hand, are notorious for accidental discharges, as you can remove the magazine but still have a round in the chamber. Accidental discharges happen over and over—and often by people who should know better.

Given a choice, I prefer a semiautomatic, as it holds more rounds. Specifically, I like Glock firearms. All Glocks work the same and only differ by caliber and therefore size. So if you can shoot one Glock, you can shoot them all. A Glock 42 is the smallest Glock and can easily fit in the front pocket of your jeans. It fires six .380 caliber rounds. From a front pocket carry, it can be quickly accessed. There are a variety of third-party pocket holsters available for the Glock 42. These are essentially sleeves that fit around your Glock when you carry it in the front pocket. Upon drawing the weapon, the sleeve sticks to the inside of your pocket as the weapon comes out. It is an excellent method of concealed carry. The .380 round is a bit small, however, in terms of power. You can achieve more stopping power with a 9mm.

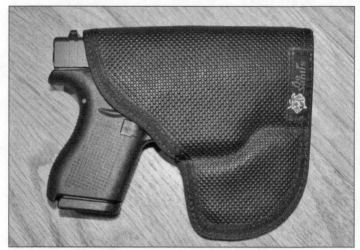

Figure 5. Glock 42 with pocket holster.

Figures 6–8. Drawing sequence from a front pocket carry.

A 9mm round packs more stopping power than a .380. For a smaller 9mm weapon, the Glock 26 is an excellent choice. It fires ten 9mm rounds but, due to the larger size, requires a different carry method. For the Glock 26, I like to use an in-the-waistband holster or a holster on my belt, wearing it back on my right hip, as it is too big to fit into the front pocket of the jeans. Once in a while, I will carry it in an appendix holster that fits on the inside of my belt in the front of my pants. This is convenient for sitting down and drawing, but the prospect of a misfire is so horrible to contemplate that I don't carry with this holster too often. Choice of wardrobe comes into play here because you need to be able to access your weapon with a variety of jackets and shirts. In this day and age, there are actually lines of clothing designed for concealed carry by companies such as 5.11 Tactical. Unfortunately for women, other than handbags, there are more concealed carry fashion choices for men. And of course, drawing from the holster with concealed carry clothing requires practice.

Finally, for maximum protection, nothing beats carrying a Glock 19 (excluding the Glock 17, of course, which holds seventeen rounds). The Glock 19 holds fifteen rounds plus one in the chamber. Due to its larger size, however, I will carry this just behind my right hip on a belt with a Serpa holster. I really like the Serpa holster brand. It has a security feature in the form of a button that requires you to depress it in order to draw the weapon; otherwise, the weapon will not come out of the holster. You can literally be upside down or someone could grab your weapon, and it will not come out of the holster without depressing that outer button. This means, of course, that you must practice drawing your weapon so that you can sweep your clothing away and draw the weapon successfully while depressing the button. And you should practice this enough so that you can do it smoothly and without thinking. In shooting we say, "Slow is smooth and smooth is fast." Practice slowly to impress each element of the draw into your muscle memory. If you practice this way enough, you will fully appreciate the adage.

Another aspect that makes the Glock brand attractive is the ability to dry fire the weapon. This means that you can take an empty Glock without the magazine, rack the slide to cock the weapon, and practice drawing the weapon, aiming at a target, and actually pulling the trigger. You will feel the trigger travel for a bit before it reaches the point of tension and finally into the point of firing. This allows you to "take up the slack" in the trigger before actually pulling it and will result in more accurate shooting. You can practice dry firing at a spot on the wall. Try putting the front site on the spot, take up the trigger slack, and squeeze the trigger. On the range, if you are seeing your shots hit to the left, you are likely anticipating the shot, or if to the right, it's probably because you are flinching or "pulling" the trigger rather than squeezing it evenly to the rear. Just like in that living hell game called golf, in which the follow-through after hitting the ball is a vital component of your swing, so too is follow-through important in shooting. For me, shooting requires a level of concentration akin to Zen meditation or Zen archery. The focus and concentration required is challenging and is also somehow refreshing.

For women, there is a large range of handbags that are made for concealed carry. In addition, there are things like ankle holsters and fanny pack–type holsters. Whichever holsters you choose, however, the important point is to practice with them. This can be problematic at some public ranges, where shooters are often not allowed to draw from the holster—much less a purse concealment or ankle holster.

Figure 9. There are a variety of concealed carry handbag options for women.

BEWARE PUBLIC RANGES

A word about public ranges. Some public ranges are atrocious. Safety rules are relaxed and you have to remain very cognizant of what the idiot sticks to your left and right are doing. You can be the most safety conscious shooter on the range, but it won't matter if the guy next to you is flagging (inadvertently waving the muzzle) at people to his left and right because he has poor muzzle discipline. Try to find a range that allows you to practice with various holsters and distances. (Most encounters with a pistol happen within five yards.) Also make sure that there is sufficient distance between shooters. Some outdoor ranges do this quite nicely.

THE ACHILLES' HEEL OF CONCEALED CARRY—DEPENDENCY

For most of my adult life, I've been involved in martial arts. In those years, I can't count the number of times I've heard someone exclaim something to the effect of: "I don't need that stuff. I'll just take out my gun and shoot 'em." These people are convinced in the strength of their argument, and there is no swaying them. The problem with this line of thinking is that it is based on a couple of inconvenient assumptions. It is assuming that you will have a firearm on you at all times. It is also assuming that you will always have time to draw and fire your weapon. So for many people, the consequence of carrying a firearm is that they will form a dependency on it. They will be tempted to go for their firearm when a forearm to the throat might be more effective. Dependency on one's firearm could be rightly described as the Achilles' heel of concealed carry—and very possibly with dangerous consequences.

Many people don't realize that a man with a knife can almost always stab a person with a holstered weapon before the man with the firearm can react. Moreover, a determined antagonist with a knife can execute such an attack from as far away as twenty-one feet. Twenty-one feet is about the distance it takes for your brain to register that you are under attack, draw your weapon, and fire it effectively. I've done this exercise, and it is eye-opening. And even at twenty-one feet, it still required me to back up as I drew my weapon and brought the front site onto the charging target. Think about that the next time you read that the police shot a man with a knife who was not complying with their instructions. Twenty-one feet—it's a hell of a long distance.

What about the woman who had a handgun in her handbag and was grabbed from behind while loading groceries into her car? Or the woman who woke up and found a man standing over her in her bedroom? A handgun didn't help there either. Weapons have a place in your defensive skills matrix, but make sure you have other options too.

A WORD ABOUT OPEN CARRY

In this day and age, it's become increasingly popular to open carry, where you walk around displaying your firearm. While I can see that under some circumstances, this could make sense, by and large, I am opposed to it. It is a form of public intimidation and therefore hard to condone. From a self-protection point of view, you are advertising what you believe is your strength. A predator will strike first and without warning, and you therefore risk losing at the outset what you consider to be your best option. The predator uses surprise to achieve his goal, and you should too. Better to go concealed.

Firearms require forethought, practice, and skill, and you

should be aware of the legal consequences of your actions, as they vary from state to state. Claiming "I shot him in self-defense" does not make it so in the eyes of the law. It is, however, an admission to killing someone. For that reason, along with the highly litigious nature of our society, joining an organization like U.S. LawShield or United States Concealed Carry Association would be prudent, as they are geared to assist in legal defense issues for clients involved in deadly force encounters. Finally, seek out quality instruction. All it takes is a momentary lapse in judgment or one poor decision, and your world could change forever—for the worse.

KEY CONCEPTS

- Active shooter situation: If you are in a room and an active shooter enters it, your best chance of survival is to fight like a sociopath and shut off his brain. Hiding at that point is an almost sure invitation to death. Hoping he will run out of ammo won't cut it. A blow to the neck with the forearm can kill or knock out the largest opponent. Injury Dynamics and Target Focus Training are two systems that emphasize this target extensively.
- Consider the implications of concealed carry for you and your family. If you choose to carry, keep your skills up. Practice slowly. (Slow is smooth and smooth is fast.)
- Consider the implications of exposing children with behavior issues to firearms—never forget the example of Adam Lanza at Sandy Hook.
- Recognize that when you carry, you could find yourself more willing to get involved in conflicts than when you don't have a weapon. If you find yourself acting that way, be honest with yourself and don't take a weapon with you.

You are simply more dangerous to yourself and others with that kind of mindset.

- Understand that dependency on your firearm is the Achilles' heel of concealed carry and of firearms in general. Learn to use other weapons, including what God gave you—your skeleton.
- If you aren't willing to take a life—and contend with all of the legal and moral consequences that go with it—don't carry a firearm.
- If you do conceal carry, in addition to keeping your skills up, consider joining something like U.S. LawShield or the United States Concealed Carry Association. These organizations provide legal defense for members involved in deadly force encounters.
- Seek out quality instruction.

10

BLADES—USING THEM AND DEFENDING AGAINST THEM

Tension between Kell and Blackmon had been simmering for weeks. The day before the murder, three prisoners at the Gunnison facility of the Utah Department of Corrections—Troy Kell, Eric Daniels, and Paul Payne—submitted medical request forms to go to the prison's medical unit. Payne submitted one more medical request form—a forgery—for their target, Lonnie Blackmon. The intent was to get Blackmon out of his cell so they could kill him.

On the day of the murder, Blackmon—to his surprise—was summoned from his cell to go to the medical unit. Kell and his target, Blackmon, were on the upper level of the building where they were housed. They were both placed in double-locked handcuffs that were attached to a belt around their waist. Their feet were shackle-free so that they could go down the stairs. Daniels, similarly restrained, had already been moved to the lower level while Payne's request was denied, as he was in isolation.

Blackmon was moved to the lower level first. As Kell descended the stairs, he took out a handcuff shim he had made and hidden in his clothing. With it, he removed his handcuffs as he was walking down the stairs. Blackmon had his back toward Kell and was talking with another prisoner. With his hands free, Kell removed the homemade shank he had also concealed in his clothes and, achieving absolute surprise, proceeded to stab Blackmon repeatedly in the neck and back. Still hand-cuffed with the cuffs attached to his waist, Blackmon stood little chance as Daniels tackled his legs and held them down while Kell stabbed Blackmon in the neck, eyes, face, back, and chest. A total of sixty-seven times over the course of two and a half minutes. Kell became so tired at one point, he actually stood up for a momentary break before he resumed his assault on Blackmon. Interestingly, the postmortem exam revealed that of the sixty-seven stabs (all captured on video), only two were deemed by the forensic examiner as being capable of inflicting death in the short term. Targeting matters.

THE EDGED WEAPON—PRIMAL AND PERSONAL

For sure, there is something primal about a knife attack. The appearance of a knife alone can cause the bravest to waver. The Gurkhas, who have achieved a fearsome reputation as professional soldiers over the last couple of centuries, have proven this time and again. They are known for their skill with the Nepalese kukri—a machete-type blade with a distinctive bend in the blade. Their reputation was so fierce that in 1982, during the Falkland Islands conflict, Argentine troops abandoned their positions rather than face the Gurkhas. They knew the legend that if a Gurkha draws his kukri, he must draw blood. Sun Tzu would have been proud to see the Gurkhas in 1982, as they achieved their victory almost on reputation alone. Today, law enforcement officers are keenly aware of the lethality of an edged weapon. While Kell's targeting left something to be desired, he clearly got the job done. There are some interesting lessons to be drawn:

- Knife attacks are vicious, brutal, and bloody. They touch a primal nerve.
- Many people who have been stabbed during a crime reported that they never saw the knife and at first thought they had been punched.
- The human body can take a lot of stabs (only two of sixty-seven of Blackmon's thrusts were considered lethal).

Program yourself, starting now, that if you get stabbed, you still have a lot of fight left in you, and your number one goal in the universe is to shut off the brain of the assailant. It is a natural human reaction to focus on the knife hand during an attack, but if you do that, you will almost always be behind the power curve. In today's world of proliferate security cameras, the internet is replete with knife attacks caught on camera. Over and over, it has been demonstrated in actual stabbings that when the victim focused on the knife, it was simply too easy for the assailant to alternate high and low thrusts—the defender's brain was always a step behind and couldn't catch up, let alone anticipate. If you are close enough to try to grapple for the knife, then you are close enough to rupture his eye with a finger, crush his throat, or rupture his testicles. And once you achieve any one of those injuries, the situation changes dramatically in your favor, and you can proceed to systematically destroy the assailant's body until he enters unconsciousness or death.

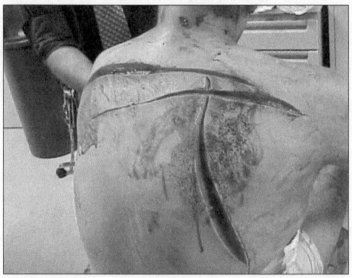

Figure 10. Stabbing is more lethal than slashing. Slashes are horrible and bloody but often survivable. Stabs affect vital organs.

FIGHTING AN ANTAGONIST WHO IS WIELDING A KNIFE

Actual stabbings are notorious for fast and furious attacks, where the antagonist overruns his target while executing multiple stabs. The predatory killer doesn't practice a style, collect chi, or study for a belt. He simply closes the distance and overwhelms his target with as many stabs in as short a time as possible—and it works really, really well. This brutal kind of attack is vastly different from what you find in martial arts schools, where one person faces off a few paces from his antagonist and makes a measured thrust at his fellow student and holds it there while the other student executes a knife disarm and then usually follows up with some kind of submission. If you think you are going to start a knife encounter on full alert and several paces away from your attacker with a few moments of hesitation followed by a single thrust by the attacker and a clever submission from you, then you are setting yourself up for failure. But this is exactly how the vast majority of martial arts schools teach knife defense. And Hollywood feeds into this falsehood by making knife fights look entertaining.

While it's unfair to make sweeping judgments about the martial arts world in general, from my experience, the vast majority of knife-disarm techniques are unrealistic and certainly can't deal with the violence of a jailhouse-style knife attack, the style of choice among killers with knives. And we already saw how a predator like Neal Beckman was disarmed of his knife and still managed to empty his revolver into the body of Sergeant Young. Sergeant Young achieved the only viable solution when he turned off Beckman's brain with two well-aimed shots.

In a lifetime of studying various styles, among the most effective combatives training at dealing with knife attacks are Injury Dynamics and Target Focus Training. Krav Maga would be another. Why? Because they essentially advocate turning off the brain of the person wielding the knife and not overly focusing on the knife itself. Going for a debilitating injury in the midst of being attacked by a person with a knife obviously requires considerable mental discipline, but you can start to ingrain it into your DNA through slow practice. Focus on achieving one injury to buy precious seconds to inflict the next injury—and the one after that followed by the one after that—until the threat is unconscious or dead. Slow deliberate practice will ingrain proper targeting. Speed will come with experience.

The following is demonstrative of the attack philosophy of Chris Ranck-Buhr, founder of Injury Dynamics and former head instructor of Target Focus Training. In violent encounters—like military or intelligence operations planning—the plan rarely survives first contact. Consequently, actions in violent encounters are not predictable. What is predictable are reactions to certain injuries; that is, a finger into the eye will cause a person to move away from the finger while covering his eye. A kick to the groin will result in a person bending over to cover their groin while jutting their chin out. A forearm strike to the neck will cause a person to step back and reach for their neck. These spinal reflexes can't be controlled any more than you can control yourself from recoiling your hand when you burn it on the stove or the doctor taps your knee to test your reflexes and your leg involuntarily moves as a result. So the "techniques," for lack of a better term, shown next are merely some of the potential options for strikes against a person wielding a knife. A practitioner of Injury Dynamics will execute a strike and look for the expected spinal reflex reaction that will indicate if the strike was successful or not. If not, time for plan B and searching for another target.

(Note the flat back foot in all of the stances.)

DEALING WITH A JAILHOUSE-STYLE KNIFE ATTACK TO THE MIDSECTION USING INJURY DYNAMICS

Figure 11. With little or no time to react, or perhaps after already having been stabbed once, execute a circle strike with your ulna bone (forearm) against the radial nerve of your antagonist. The radial nerve is against the bone about midlength on the inside of the forearm. A solid strike is often enough to cause a person to drop whatever they are holding. The key is to stay close to your antagonist, which may feel counterintuitive and, therefore, must be ingrained in training.

Figure 12. Stepping through or past him to engage your body weight, insert as much finger into the eye as possible. This will cause your antagonist to move back away from his injury.

Figure 13. While your antagonist is contemplating his vision, go for a field goal using your shin or ball of your foot to his groin.

Figure 14. While he is bent over contemplating his groin, strike the neck with your forearm as you step through or past him to engage your body weight.

Figure 15. When he is on the ground, you have time to pick your next target. In this instance, stomping the ankle and breaking both the ankle bone and toes presents an inviting target and will take away his ability to walk.

Overhead knife attacks occur more in horror movies than in real life. But in the event you were ever faced with such an occurrence, Injury Dynamics offers a potential counter.

Figure 16. Up-circle strike with forearm to his radial nerve. Grab and pull the knife hand while striking the solar plexus with the point of the elbow. Note the deep stance and the action of pulling his balance while striking.

Figure 17. Continue to pull his balance while striking the ribs as you shuffle through him.

Figure 18. Continue to shuffle into his center of gravity while pulling the knife hand. Grab a fistful of groin and "start the lawn mower."

Figure 19. Using the web of your hand, strike and grab the throat.

Figure 20. Hang on to the throat and add a hammer fist to the hinge of the jaw. Step deeply and maintain structure to engage your body weight. Once he is on the ground, you can choose your next target, like a stomp to the ankle or kick to the groin.

One point of clarification is in order. It's easy to look at martial arts books or the photos presented here and lose sight of the fact that, in most cases, if you are attacked by an experienced antagonist wielding a knife, your prognosis for seeing another day on the planet will be severely hampered. He will attempt to achieve complete tactical surprise and will try to overwhelm you with as many stabs in as short a time frame as possible. You will need to push through the denial/deliberation phase in fractions of a second to get to action. And that action must be solely focused on shutting off the brain of your antagonist. And the fastest path to that happy ending will be to injure your antagonist so that he goes on the defensive while you commence to commit serial injury. If you focus on trying to intercept the knife hand and wrestle/disarm/submit your opponent, the chances of living to tell the tale will be highly diminished.

OFFENSIVE KNIFE WORK AND THE LIBRE KNIFE FIGHTING SYSTEM

During World War II, operators in the Office of Strategic Services, the precursor to the modern-day CIA, received offensive knife training from British Major W. E. Fairbairn. A legacy in the special operations community, Fairbairn served in the Shanghai Municipal Police in the early part of the twentieth century and was a practitioner of Kodokan jujitsu. He studied kung fu under Tsai Ching Tung, who at one time was employed at the imperial palace in Beijing as in instructor to retainers of the empress dowager. He designed a knife for commandos and the OSS in World War II, which can be seen at the CIA's museum in headquarters. While offensive knife fighting is largely a lost art for the CIA in modern times, there are a handful of skilled knife fighters walking the planet. One of them is Scott Babb. Scott is a soft-spoken and thoughtful conversationalist. He enjoys philosophy and can quote Machiavelli and Shakespeare. His calm persona belies his unique skill in knife fighting, and there is no doubt he could fillet you like a fish in seconds if he ever felt that he needed to. He is the creator of the Libre Knife Fighting Guild based in San Diego, and his fighting style is now practiced in cities all over the world. As skilled in instruction as he is a practitioner, Scott has put together a highly functional knife fighting system with none of the frills and ceremony that accompany so many martial arts in our day. If you think that you would like to learn how to attack with a knife, there is no better reference than Libre.

If you are going to carry a knife, then you first need to consider how brutal and bloody a knife encounter will be and prepare yourself mentally. Stabbing someone in the neck or slashing an eye takes considerable forethought. Targeting is important if you want to avoid having to stab someone sixty-seven times. Then consider what kind of knife. Fixed blade is better than folded, as it is easier to deploy.

KNIFE IN THE ATTACK

Physically, attacking is easy. (Mentally, the act of stabbing someone in the neck or eye requires a certain amount of intent.) Using the ice-pick grip, the attack should make maximum use of the element of surprise and overwhelm your target with sudden and debilitating violence. Your targets should be the neck and/or the eyes. Practice slowly, and with time, your execution will become much faster while maintaining proper targeting. By having your forearm parallel to the ground, you afford yourself the opportunity to clear a left- or right-hand block made by your opponent. You should step into and through your target to get your body weight engaged in the strike. Each strike should be rapidly thrust and pulled out immediately in order to set up the next thrust, with the goal of doubling over your opponent. Once doubled over, you will be in the strongest position to prosecute your attack in the most efficient manner possible.

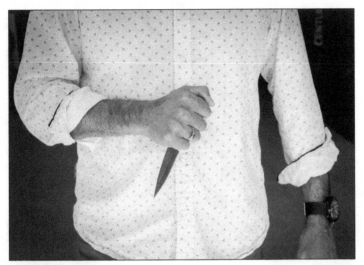

Figure 21. The ice-pick grip.

Figure 22. Preattack posture.

Figure 23. Attack posture.

Libre Knife Fighting and Injury Dynamics can be combined offensively as demonstrated in figures 24–29.

Figure 24. With the striking arm parallel to the deck, strike for the neck.

Figure 25. In spite of the block, the attacker checks the blocking arm at the elbow and gets a stab to the neck.

Figure 26: The attack to the neck forces your opponent to bend over and cover his wound—which is where you want him.

Figure 27: Quickly strike as many targets as possible.

Figure 28: Execute an ankle stomp. Aim above the nob of the ankle and stomp through to the center of his stance (as if you were stomping the biggest, nastiest, centipede on earth).

Figure 29: Add an extra stomp—in this instance to the ankle. In practice, move slowly with control. But in your mind, "make the can flat."

Does executing such violence seem cold and callous? Absolutely. Would I like to do this to another human being? Absolutely not—the thought is abhorrent. If my wife or child's life were at stake, would I execute this? As brutally and efficiently as possible.

Learning to fight like a sociopath does not make you a sociopath, but it will certainly enable you to defeat one if the situation calls for it. Better to play it out several thousand times in training and never have to use it than to be forced to think about it for the first time during your moment of truth. And if you never have to resort to such base brutality, congratulations, you beat the odds. But if someday the stars align to place you into such a predicament, you will have already experienced a multitude of similar situations on the practice mats—and your ability to reach into your experiences and achieve a solution could very well save your life.

KNIFE LAWS VARY—KNOW THEM

Like gun laws, knife laws vary from state to state. In many cases, they are stricter than gun laws, particularly when it comes to concealed carry. In addition, many of the laws are accompanied by vague language that is open to interpretation (by the courts, not you). Blade length and type of blade matter. In war zones, I always carried a fixed blade as a last resort backup weapon (fortunately never having to use it). And I trained almost daily with a colleague. But domestically, the rules for fixed blades are more stringent than folding knives. Bottom line: understand the laws of your state (and sometimes the law even varies from city to city within the same state).

FOLDING KNIVES, KRAMBITS, AND THE HAZARDS OF A RING GRIP

Laws regarding folding knives are the most lenient laws in the knife realm, and there are some fearsome looking folding knives on the market. But knives and guns share the same unique problem. If you carry a knife, then you are likely going to form a dependency on it. And if your go-to knife is a folding knife, then you have to practice deploying it on the draw. There are a variety of folding knives and folding krambits on the market. Lately, a design has emerged on some knives that features a notch on the blade so that if you draw it correctly from your pocket, the notch catches on the pocket itself and opens by the time you have the knife in front of you. This requires continuous practice (and a few sets of pants as the pockets get torn up) to ensure that in your moment of crisis you will have a fully deployed knife. You can imagine the results if you think the knife has fully deployed but, in reality, is still in midfold. If you tried to stab someone with that blade you would only succeed in probably cutting one of your fingers off. Not a great way to start a fight for your life.

Krambits from Southeast Asia are evil looking and popular among Southeast Asian martial artists. Manufactures and proponents of krambits will show impressive demonstrations of them slicing through hanging meat. You can't help but be impressed. However, one consideration for any knife with a ring grip, including most krambits, is that experience has shown that blades with a ring grip can cause injury to the finger in the ring if the blade gets stuck in bone.

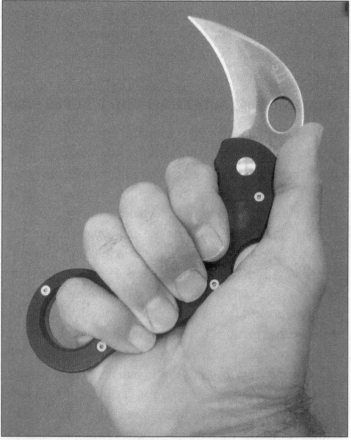

Figure 30. The krambit, from Southeast Asia, is a fearsome-looking weapon. But consider the implications of any knife with a ring grip, as it could cause problems if you penetrate bone.

FIXED BLADES—LESS TO WORRY ABOUT

My preference is for a fixed blade. With a fixed blade, you never have to worry if the knife deployed properly or not. That is one less thing to go wrong in a violent confrontation. At the same time, the laws governing dirks can be both vague and strict, and you will want to know what they are for your state as well as blade length limitations. Strangely, open carry is often allowed, but concealed carry could cause you problems legally.

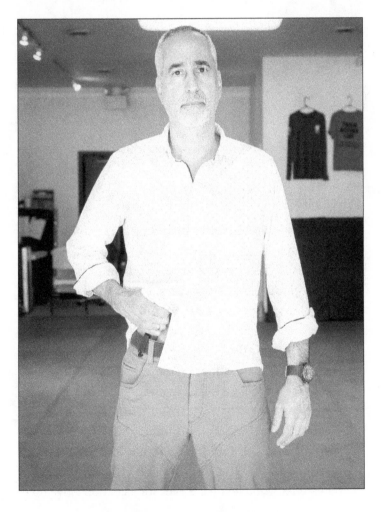

Figures 31 and 32. Fixed blades deploy without having to worry if the blade is open or not—unlike a folding knife. Deployment must be practiced regularly as with a firearm to achieve a smooth and effective draw with a variety of clothing.

KEY CONCEPTS

- Fixed blades are superior to folding blades for a violent encounter.
- Knife laws are often stricter than gun laws, particularly laws regarding concealed carry. Understand the laws of your state and city, as they may vary.
- If you want to learn how to use a knife offensively, look up Scott Babb and Libre Knife Fighting System, based in San Diego, California. While you are at it, join Injury Dynamics, also in San Diego, either online or in person, if you are fortunate enough to live near Southern California.
- Victims of stabbing report thinking they were initially punched and only later realized they had been stabbed. Also, understand that the human body can take a lot of punishment, and if you are ever stabbed, don't give up!

- Accept that knife fights are primal and bloody—very bloody (the average person has five to seven quarts of blood circulating in their body).
- If you are using a knife offensively, targeting counts! Understand that people almost never get stabbed once and simply fall down. You will need to pursue targets until they are unconscious or dead.
- If you are fighting a person who has a knife, your only goal is to turn off their brain. Don't get fixated on the knife hand. You will always be behind the curve if you do.
- Practice using a knife offensively, employing a slow practice methodology and gradually ramping up speed with experience and ability. It is equally important that you visualize the violence of the attack; make each practice session count. You can always be a civilized human being (and hopefully that is your default state of being). But you have to train—mentally and physically—to fight like a sociopath in order to defeat a sociopath.

11

IMPROVISED WEAPONS: MUSINGS AND RECOMMENDATIONS

THE PSYCHOLOGICAL DISADVANTAGE OF ANY WEAPON

Dependency on your "go-to" weapon will place you at a terrible psychological disadvantage if you ever find yourself in a life-or-death situation without it. To avoid dependency on any one weapon, it is useful to be familiar with multiple weapons and to include your bare hands, which you will never be without. The more familiar you are with a variety of weapons, the more your brain will be able to respond in a crisis, as it will have a greater wealth of experience to draw from.

While knowing how to defend yourself with just your body is obviously a great advantage, there is also little doubt that having something in hand that can increase leverage, reach, and lethality is also greatly advantageous. Knives and guns are great, but what if you don't have them when fate comes knocking? Or you are overseas, where such weapons are illegal? Enter the improvised weapon.

For improvised weapons, there is an almost infinite number of choices. Some—such as flinging a pocketful of coins at the face or the old Chinese mafia tactic of throwing ground glass into the eyes of an opponent—are designed to distract and injure. But for our purposes, we will look at using improvised weapons for more practical purposes: for use in the worst fifteen seconds of the worst day of your life—when everything is on the line.

But there are three principles required for any weapon—improvised or otherwise—to be effective:

1. The targeting of the strike must be accurate. A finger or improvised weapon to the eye is hugely effective. Hit an inch too high, however, and you strike the forehead—which achieves nothing.
2. The strike itself must have sufficient penetrating power to ensure the debilitation of your target. Employing your body weight into the strike makes it most effective. But there are three targets that you can still injure without employing body weight: the eyes, throat, and groin.
3. To achieve 1 and 2 requires forethought and practice.

FIRST, DITCH THE MACE

Many women opt to carry Mace (a brand name of a type of pepper spray). I don't recommend Mace, as it has several drawbacks. First off, if you are going to carry something for protection, you need to practice with it. Most owners never do this with Mace, part of the reason being the high cost of replacing a single-use item. The other deterrent is that you just can't go around spraying pepper spray in public in order to practice. So the result is that the spray often remains on the woman's key chain for extended periods of time and usually well past the expiration date of the product. Usually, the first time it is ever used is at the time of the most critical need. It would be like giving a gun to someone who never shot a firearm, expecting them to deploy the weapon successfully in their moment of truth. In that time of critical need, when the heart is pounding and motor skills are degraded, a good number of people will not deploy the spray correctly and either miss their target or inadvertently spray themselves.

Moreover, in a violent encounter, you need to inflict injury, and that means taking something away from your antagonist. Crush the testicles, and you take away his ability to breathe or move. Insert a finger in the eye, and you take away his ability to see. Crush his windpipe with your forearm, and you take away his ability to breathe. Stomp through a knee or ankle, and you take away his ability to walk.

Pepper spray is an irritant and will not cause an injury. We are *not* trying to inflict pain. Not everyone has the same tolerance for pain, and different people will react to pain differently. Mace may be debilitating for one person or a mere inconvenience for another. An attacker can be in pain and still do you great harm. Or worse, he can be in a drug-, alcohol-, or adrenaline-induced rage and not feel the spray at all. Go for the injury instead.

CIA operations officers routinely travel abroad, often in unstable and dangerous environments. Situational awareness usually sees us through the day when navigating these locales.

But it never hurts to have a little extra insurance. So let's look at a couple of options.

THE LOWLY SCREWDRIVER

It's true that James Bond never had to resort to carrying a screwdriver. But then he never had to contend with an army of lawyers at headquarters or squeamish bureaucrats more concerned over their own career management than the safety of their officers either. Enter the screwdriver. You can buy one legally anywhere in the world. Having one in your possession can always be explained whether you are in Jakarta, Khartoum, Karachi, New York, or Tokyo. They have good grips and, held in the fist point down, can constitute a highly effective stabbing weapon. Slashing weapons like certain knives or the Southeast Asian krambit create horrible looking wounds but won't necessarily prove fatal. Insert a four-inch screwdriver through the ribs, however, and damage to internal organs will be lethal. Glamorous? Not a bit. Effective? You can bet your life on it. Think "eyes, throat, groin," and repeat as necessary until satisfied.

HANG ON TO THAT COPY OF *WOMEN'S HEALTH!*

Another excellent option that doesn't involve stabbing is the innocuous magazine. Some countries and some cities have very strict concealed carry laws for firearms and edged weapons, but none of them ban carrying a magazine. If you simply roll up a magazine as tightly as you can and tie the rolled magazine with women's hairbands on each end and the middle, you now have an extremely hard baton. A single strike to the side of the neck will easily cause an electrical knockout. A two-handed grip with a strike to the front of the throat would have a lethal result. A rolled magazine will fit easily in a handbag, car, jacket pocket, or even back pocket of a pair of jeans.

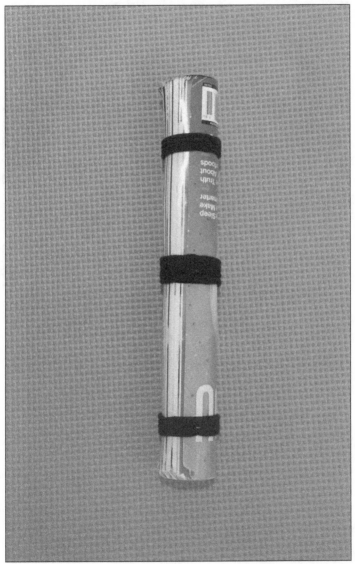

Figure 33. Any magazine rolled up tightly and tied with hairbands becomes a formidable weapon. Laminated covers like those found on some fashion magazines are even harder.

Figures 34 and 35. Drawing the magazine from the back pocket. Good targets are the front and back of the neck for a lethal strike and the sides of the neck for a knockout. You can also attack the eyes and groin.

Figures 36 and 37. After clubbing your antagonist in the neck "like a baby seal," execute an ankle stomp. Now that he is debilitated, you can pick another target or leave without worry he will follow.

THE MIGHT OF A PEN

Imagine for a moment that you skipped over the part in this book that discussed knowing your car and knowing how and when your cars doors lock. You get in the car and start the ignition, forgetting to lock your door. At that moment, your passenger door opens and a man gets inside. You instinctively grab the pen in the center console that you bought on discount at Staples last week and, holding it in your fist in an ice-pick grip, start with alternating strikes of the eyes, throat, and groin. The chances of you breaking something on your antagonist in those opening moments are extremely high. You can get a sense of the punching power you can generate with a pen by setting up a martial arts kick bag (one that you don't mind poking holes in) on your passenger seat in your car or even on your sofa. Then from the driver's seat or adjacent seat on your sofa, start stabbing. You will be pleasantly surprised at the effectiveness of this technique. And while using your body weight is ideal, when strapped into the front seat of the car, this will do. There are also a variety of commercial pens that are made from metal and made precisely for self-defense.

THE KEY DEFENSE

There are numerous documented examples of women using a key in the fist to successfully strike an assailant. But like everything, there are pros and cons to consider. The pros are that this can clearly work—if you hit the right target. You will want to destroy someone's eye or throat with this. Nothing wrong with that, but you have to mentally prepare yourself before you find yourself in a critical situation. You have to come to grips with the fact that you will put your entire effort into destroying the eyes of someone assaulting you. And while necessity can indeed be the mother of invention, your chances of success will be much higher if you commit to this before those critical fifteen seconds. Like the pro golfer who visualizes every aspect of his swing, ball flight, and target on the green, so too must you visualize how you would hold the key and exactly where you will strike. If you think a knife is primal, this takes primal to a whole new level. So mentally prepare. You can practice by moving slowly with a Bob dummy or even just shadowbox in front of a mirror. Practice slowly and deliberately, and try it again with a training partner. Pause just in front of his eyes (as blinding your training partner with your keys would not be cool) and then just imagine completing the act. Do it until you are bored.

One thing I don't like about the key defense is that you will need those keys to presumably drive away or get into your home. Injured people move away from the point of injury, so you might find yourself losing your grip on your keys as your target moves back from the injury and possibly losing your keys in the process.

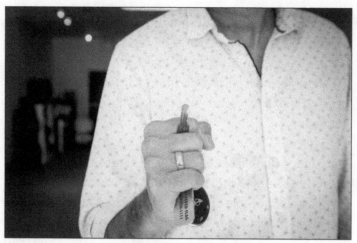

Figures 38 and 39. Keys in the fist can work well, especially against the eyes and throat.

FLASHLIGHTS

An excellent alternative to the key defense is using a flashlight. SureFire makes some excellent lights that are so bright they will momentarily blind an opponent. They are made of hard steel, and some have beveled edges, which will magnify any injury when used as a stabbing instrument. Aim for alternating strikes to the eyes, throat, and groin. They are small enough to carry anywhere, including overseas, and are extremely useful for just the light itself in the event of a car crash or power outage.

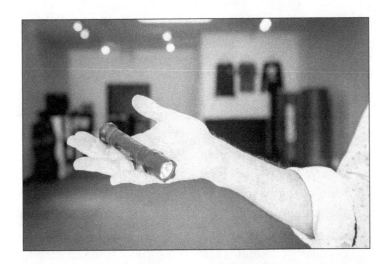

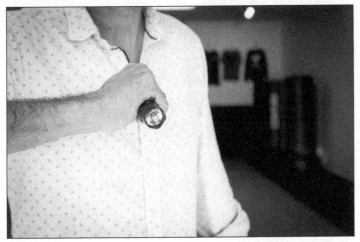

Figures 40 and 41. Grip for flashlight defense. Your targets are the eyes, throat, and groin—repeat as necessary.

KEY CONCEPTS

- Improvised weapons can be just as lethal as real weapons. But in order to work, they require you to strike your target accurately and with force. The magazine with hairbands will drop a man if you strike him in the neck, but if your targeting is off by a couple of inches, you will strike the shoulder and have almost no effect.

- Don't let an actual emergency be the first time you try one of these techniques. Bring them all into your quiver by practicing with each improvised weapon. You can shadowbox the strikes and then practice slowly with a partner.
- Prepare yourself mentally. Visualize each strike in your mind's eye. History is replete with women victims who were strangled to death while they scratched the face of their attacker. Had they just committed to inserting their finger into the eye of the attacker, the outcome would have been very different. This is an asocial act, so you have to prepare yourself mentally and then commit to doing it with an improvised weapon or simply your hand.

12

GOING MANO A MANO-FIGHTING WITH YOUR HANDS

MARTIAL ARTS SCHOOLS AND COMPETITIONS

Who can resist watching a bout of mixed martial arts (MMA)? These athletes appear to be competing in the ultimate struggle. They are supremely fit and fearsome in appearance. The pressure is intense, the stakes are high, and the competition is fast, brutal, and exciting to watch. What these competitors endure in the Octagon is highly admirable by any standard. Their training necessitates expertise in various styles, is intensive and all-consuming, and requires tremendous endurance and dedication. Brazilian jujitsu, in particular, took the Octagon by storm and was propelled by the popular adage that "all fights end up on the ground." Now comes the caveat. The realm in which MMA skills are best suited is where we see it: in competition. Competition with defined rules forces the contestants onto a level playing field where they can bring the attributes we admire to the fore: strength, ability, endurance, sacrifice, technique, and fortitude. To level the field and force those attributes, MMA has a host of rules to promote safety and fair competition. Among them, you can't:

- Eye gouge.
- Spike an opponent to the canvas on his head or neck.
- Strike the spine or the back of the head.
- Strike the throat and/or grab the trachea.
- Stretch your fingers toward an opponent's face/eyes.
- Strike downward with your elbow.
- Attack the groin.
- Knee and/or kick the head of a grounded opponent.
- Stomp a grounded opponent.
- Manipulate a small joint.

MMA would lose its luster if one contestant executed a shoot to the legs of the other and took him to the mat, and the recipient of that takedown sank his thumb to the knuckle into the eye of his antagonist. All of the admirable attributes are suddenly rendered moot, and the match is over.

Many people believe that if they train in MMA or other styles, then they can just tweak the basic principles to make it lethal. I agree that is possible, but only if the practitioner incorporates those lethal aspects into their training so that they will do it without thinking if ever called upon to do so. Ask the MMA practitioner whose antagonist tapped out and then promptly shot him when the submission was relaxed. We default to our training under pressure, and in competitive sports, we respect the tap out as a signal that your antagonist has given up. But in street violence, there is no tapping out.

At a training course I once attended, we looked at a case study of an officer who properly employed deadly force when he and another American were targeted by a terrorist organization for kidnapping. They were in a barber shop when two armed al Qaeda fighters entered, one with an AK-47 and the other with a taser. It didn't end well for the kidnappers that day; apparently God was not willing to entertain their cause, as they were both shot to death. Interestingly, the officer who instantly assessed the situation and decisively employed deadly force immediately holstered his weapon after shooting the two terrorist would-be kidnappers—exactly the way he had done so often at the range. Shoot and holster. Shoot and holster. We default to our training.

ESTABLISH YOUR GOAL: CULTURE, COMPETITION, OR VISITING VIOLENCE ON ANOTHER HUMAN BEING?

So you need to identify what it is you are trying to get out of your training because, for sure, all martial arts are not created equally. Moreover, training in martial arts is not the same as training for violence. Modern-day martial arts have largely lost their martial utility, as we are no longer weaponless farmers or landowners confronting sword-bearing samurai. The result is an emphasis on health, athleticism, or cultural training. And while there is some utility for violence in modern martial arts, most strip-mall schools fall short in preparing you for true violence. Training for violence is much more comprehensive and includes mindset, situational awareness, first aid, employing violence of action, weapons, a study of human anatomy, and more. Training for violence is not particularly socially acceptable because it forces us to think about the unthinkable, and in a violent encounter, we are (or should be) the ones engaging in unfettered violence. If your mindset is defense, then you are already behind the power curve. In violence, we judge our success on how efficiently we visit violence upon another human being. And we may not like what we see in ourselves (and that too requires training so that we can be at peace with the consequences of our actions).

More than at any time in the past, you can find a plethora of choices for martial arts schools, and the advent of the internet has increased the choices tenfold. Many so-called experts make fantastical claims. For a really good time, do an internet search of people who purport to fling and defeat attackers with their ki and achieve a "no-touch knockout." Sifting through the chaff is no easy proposition, so what should you consider? If the no-touch knockout or winning at the man dance is your goal, thanks for reading this far; you can skip the rest of the book. If you want to compete, MMA is the perfect vehicle. If you want to learn how to grapple and to make people submit, Brazilian jujitsu is at the top of the list. There is a popular saying in martial arts circles that fights always "end up on the ground."

For sure, the vast preponderance of MMA and social encounters do end up on the ground. But if a predator has his way, only you will end up on the ground, and injured to boot as he proceeds to stomp the life out of you. If inner peace is your thing, maybe Tai Chi or aikido. Want to get flexible? Try Tae Kwon Do or the Northern China styles of kung fu. Want a cultural experience with some martial applicability? Try kung fu or silat. A little more practical and combat oriented? Consider Krav Maga or some of the harder styles of karate and kung fu. ("Harder" in this instance refers to styles that emphasize power in striking.) In many martial arts, practitioners possess tremendous athleticism and are amazing to watch. They require a high degree of endurance, flexibility, and strength, and there is little doubt as to the physical and mental health value of such systems, and usually, there are a couple of nuggets of gold to be found along the way. However, their practicality in the face of brutal violence is often left wanting. Why? Because training for modern martial arts is completely different than training for violence.

In social violence (easily identified by two males vying for dominance or territory), both sides ratchet up the tension until one launches his attack; that is, one ape hits the other. It is rarely lethal (but it can be if the attacking ape decides to hit his target with a bone or similar object, or the stricken ape hits his head on the concrete). But social violence is absolutely avoidable. It just takes one party to walk away. Even if the other apes whoop and howl, the confrontation is avoided.

Real violence, on the other hand, is unpredictable and most often catches the recipient by complete surprise. Real violence is stomach-churning and brutally effective. The person visiting violence upon another is the winner; the recipient is the loser. Jailhouse shank attacks don't happen with one inmate slowly stabbing one time and waiting for the other inmate to react twice as fast. In a real stabbing, an attacker with a knife or a homemade shiv overwhelms and overruns his victim, employing surprise and multiple stabs in as short a time frame as possible. This is territory that the sociopathic predator knows well and understands. It is not really martial and there is no art involved at all. But it works.

I've taken training where the instructors wore thick pads all over their heads and bodies. A lot of self-defense classes use these props. In my class, we were attacked with knives that emitted electric shocks when they touched you. The concept behind the pad is that you can hit them with force due to the padding. And while that is true to a point, I don't think that kind of training provides a realistic training scenario because you still cannot kick someone in the groin or hit them in the throat, or attack their eyes, and if you do, they won't feel it or, at the very least, won't react to it realistically. And if they don't react realistically, you won't get a sense of what you should expect to see with that kind of strike. That kind of training is useful in terms of experiencing a ramped-up adrenaline rush and time pressure to do something, but I wouldn't recommend it as a centerpiece of training.

Now, if you decide you want to train for violence, the absolute first condition is you must decide—in no uncertain terms—that you are willing to break and possibly kill another human being with your hands should your life or the life of your family depend on it. Period. Predators don't do styles or katas, take inner journeys, chase colored belts, or engage in chi breathing exercises. They do know what works: achieving surprise, proximity to their target, and employing overwhelming violence. We must learn what predators already know. So if you want to learn to commit no-holds-barred violence, then the field of choices narrows considerably.

Man possesses an innate ability to adapt and improve, and every generation produces its cadre of exceptional and inspirational leaders. Witness what was accomplished with airplanes from when Wilbur and Orville Wright started in 1903 to the luxurious passenger jets of today. Or the evolution of the computer, the telephone, and the internet in the last forty years. Or in a darker sense, what man has accomplished over the course of the past century in the conduct of warfare against his fellow human beings. With the possible exception of rock-

and-roll music, which has clearly taken a step backward, man's ability to improve what came before is remarkable.

The realm of hand-to-hand combat is no exception, and every generation produces a select few who are gifted in the realm of violence and even fewer who are effective at teaching it. Enter Chris Ranck-Buhr, formally of Target Focus Training (TFT) and more recently, the creator of Injury Dynamics. A prodigy of a martial arts generation, Chris teaches otherwise sane and socially responsible people how to fight like a sociopath when the situation calls for it.

INJURY DYNAMICS, TFT, AND SCARS

Luck favors the prepared mind.

—LOUIS PASTEUR

Chris is a humble, unassuming, and extraordinarily articulate instructor. He specializes in how to break the human body. His teachings focus on just about everything that mixed martial arts rules prohibit—groin attacks, eye pokes, neck attacks, stomping, and joint attacks designed to break, tear, and grind sinew and bone. He is affectionately known as "the violence whisperer" among certain circles and can just as easily discuss Russian novelist Fyodor Dostoevsky as he can describe breaking the ribs with enough force to lacerate the internal organs—sometimes in the same sentence.

Chris began his journey in San Diego with Jerry Peterson, founder of the Special Combat Aggressive Reactionary Systems (SCARS) in the early 1990s. SCARS was later adopted by the Navy Special Warfare Command through the influence of another SCARS student, Tim Larkin. Tim and Chris went on to form Target Focus Training (TFT), and from 2002 to 2017, Chris was the lead instructor for TFT, which took the SCARS concepts and expanded the system into the international and domestic markets with a newer business model, in essence introducing the system to the masses as afforded by the reach of the internet. Chris's unique ability to articulate concepts and teach in the truest sense of the word made TFT a success. In 2017, Chris and another early SCARS student and TFT instructor, Matt Suitor, established Injury Dynamics in San Diego, California.

All the strikes that are prohibited in competitive martial arts are precisely the skills Injury Dynamics teaches—in spades. Break one thing, and then begin to commit serial injury until the threat is neutralized. Injury Dynamics stresses using your body weight with every strike. What this means is that instead of striking from arm's length as taught in so many martial arts and competitive sports, you step through or past your target, thereby overrunning your target and getting your body weight involved in the strike. Instead of merely jabbing an eye from an arm's-length away, you move with your body through or past the objective, attempting to reach an imaginary point three feet behind your opponent's eye. Groin strikes, eye strikes, neck and throat strikes, tearing joints, stomping, and knee drops are all part of Injury Dynamics' repertoire.

In addition, Injury Dynamics teaches that certain strikes elicit predictable spinal reflexes (as does TFT and SCARS). For example, when you touch a hot stove, you retract your hand. You can't control this response any more than when the doctor tests your reflexes and strikes your knee with a hammer, and your knee moves in response. It is predicable. Injury Dynamics practitioners study and understand these reflexes. Any member of the male species can attest to the effects of a strike to the groin: the person struck bends over, covers his crotch, and juts out his chin. This response is absolutely predictable. If the target exhibits the expected spinal reflex, this sets up the next strike and the one after that, and the one following. If the expected spinal reflex is not observed, then the practitioner knows her intended strike failed and goes for the next strike in order to "break one thing." After that thing is broken, serial injury ensues until the threat is mitigated to your satisfaction.

Finally, unique in the martial arts world but common in Injury Dynamics, TFT, and SCARS, is the execution of slow practice, as discussed earlier in this book. The principle is that through slow practice, striking accuracy is maximized. If you practice 200 times slowly and accurately in the school, then when confronted with a real situation, the likelihood of striking effectively and accurately is vastly increased. Conversely, if you focus on speed before you have accurate targeting, you will simply reinforce poor targeting and ingrain bad habits. You don't want the first time you have to initiate a strike from your back on the ground to be the time your life depends on getting it right. Rather, slow, meticulous practice in the school is the time to work out problems related to leverage and balance. Like the pilot training for contingencies, when we are confronted with unexpected violence, our brains will search for a solution from our past experiences. For most people, if there is nothing to draw on, panic ensues. In Injury Dynamics, speed develops with experience, but the pace goes only as fast as accuracy and reaction from your training partner permits.

One other interesting aspect to Injury Dynamics is that Chris essentially teaches you to look at violence in an academic sense; that is, when studying violent confrontations, look at what worked. Don't get wrapped up in the background of the conflict. Learn from what worked and save your empathy for another time. It is akin to a medical student studying a cadaver to understand how the body works rather than getting wrapped up in the life of the person they are working on. If you run a Google search on "knockout" or "KO," you will find hundreds of examples of violence. You will notice that the person who inflicted the first real injury won every time (or as Confederate Civil War General Nathan Bedford Forrest is reputed to have said: "the firstest with the mostest" wins). You will also notice that the most effective knockouts are when the winner is very close or stepping through the loser while striking a vital target. You are learning to fight like a sociopath or an asocial predator. They know from experience what we good citizens have to learn: to injure someone, you have to have intend to harm, and you must be close—uncomfortably close for the normal person—or in the case of an Injury Dynamics practitioner, through and past your opponent.

When you study violence in an academic sense and practice violence the way Chris teaches it, you will start to build a body of experience that you can draw upon should you ever need it. You will understand that rather than move back and attempt to "defend" yourself, the best path to survival is attacking and breaking one thing (or as the famed German General Erwin Rommel stated: "the best defense is a strong offense.") For a woman, the ideal is to attack and injure before you are attacked. Don't wait until he grabs, hits, or attacks you. But this could also mean if you wake up one night and find a 220-pound man on top of you, you may have to wait for your chance to strike—tactical patience. But at some juncture, that man will reach down to unbuckle his belt or tear your clothing, and that is when you insert as much of your finger into his eye as possible with the goal of pushing your hand out of the back of his head. This will break one thing (his vision) and allow you the luxury of time to choose your next target and the one after that.

It is a profound thing to think of putting your finger deeply into someone's eye or crushing their testicles so that they are completely and irreparably ruptured. For a sane and law-abiding member of society, it is a repulsive thought almost too hard to contemplate. Through Chris's training paradigm, however, you will have thought about this and executed it hundreds of times and, therefore, gained an experiential reference in a time of need. Would you rather take your chances by not training and hoping you will never have to execute such an attack? Or would it be better to visualize and practice your actions hundreds of times and maybe never use them? Which do you suppose stands a greater chance for success in your moment of truth?

A word about ethics and morality. Practitioners of TFT and Injury Dynamics train for life-and-death situations—the realm of asocial violence. Everything else in life is essentially a social confrontation of egos and dominance. These confrontations can all be avoided and walked away from, albeit with bruised egos at times. Practitioners of Injury Dynamics and TFT understand this and, more importantly, live it.

Injury Dynamics stresses all of the hits not allowed by competitive martial arts. See the examples in Figures 42–54.

Figure 42. Neck strikes are standard fare in Injury Dynamics and are highly effective. Strikes to the front and back of the neck are potentially lethal; strikes to the side of the neck will result in a knockout if executed properly. Use your ulna bone (forearm) to make the strike while stepping through or past your opponent to maximize your body weight in the strike.

Figure 43. Groin strikes of every variety are practiced extensively. Groin strikes from various positions, such as on your feet, hands, and knees; on your back; and everything in between are practiced extensively.

Eye gouging from every conceivable position is also practiced extensively.

Figure 44. Eye gouges.

Figure 45. Stomping an opponent when he is down or occupied with a prior injury works well. In this example, the antagonist is distracted with a prior injury, so a stomp through the ankle is designed to break it.

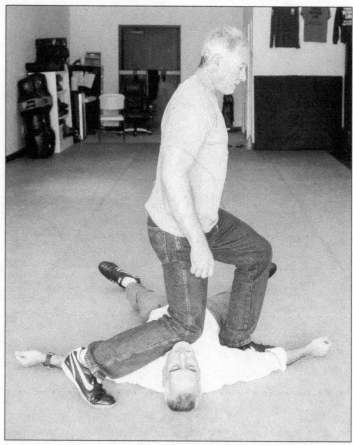

Figure 46. A knee drop to the neck is potentially lethal. Note the straight spine of the attacker.

Fight from where you find yourself.

—CHRIS RANCK-BUHR

In Injury Dynamics, practitioners will practice attacks from various positions. As Chris points out, in asocial violence, the first clue you might have that you are in a lethal situation is after you've already been struck and you find yourself on the ground. Consequently, practitioners learn to attack from the ground: on their hands and knees, on their backs, and everything in between. You learn to fight from where you find yourself.

A good rule of thumb if you find yourself on the ground is "Groin, groin, groin!" (I can hear Chris's direction just writing those words.) That means the first strike will be to the groin to obtain that first injury. If you can strike the groin with an arm, hand, elbow, shin, foot, head—whatever—then you will buy yourself precious moments to break the next thing and the one after that.

Figures 47 and 48. From your back, strike the groin.

Figure 49. After a groin strike, we can follow up with an ankle attack using the top of the shin. Cross the T with the top of your shin bone over the knob on his ankle and ride it down into the concrete.

Figure 50. In practice, disperse your weight with your hands, but on the street, all of your weight would finish on his ankle.

From your hands and knees, the principles remain the same. Attack the groin to create an injury and buy time to select your subsequent target as illustrated.

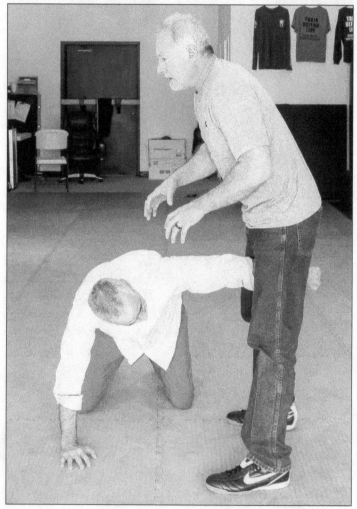

Figure 51. From the ground, strike the groin with the forearm.

Figure 52. While he is distracted with the groin attack, attack the ankle (in this example, from the inside of the leg).

Figure 53. Ride the ankle down.

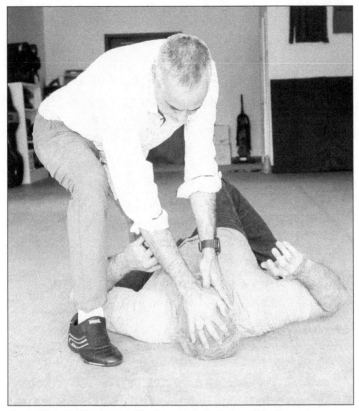

Figure 54. In fighting for your life, there are to limitations. Take the eye.

PINNED AND ON YOUR BACK? WAIT...AND STRIKE

Women, in particular, should hone their ability to learn tactical patience. If they are overwhelmed by their attacker, they may have to wait for the right time to strike. That is to say, if you are pinned on your back or being picked up from behind, at some point, your assailant will attempt to strike you, throw you down, or conduct a sexual assault. In a sexual assault, he will have to use one hand to strike or to tear your clothes or unbuckle his belt and pants. That is your moment to strike his eye, trachea, or groin (in any order that suits). You can practice this with a training partner. Have him hold you in a pin and then periodically lift a hand as if to strike you or unbutton his trousers, and then you strike the eyes or throat immediately. Do this without inducing stress to imprint the mechanics, and you can ramp up the stress level as your comfort and targeting improves over time.

Another option if pinned is to attack his balance. But you need to experiment and practice with a training partner—preferably one who is bigger and stronger than you. When you practice, have your partner pin down your arms tightly against the floor. You will notice that while you cannot lift your arms up (like in a bench-press motion), you can slide one or both arms in the direction of your head or slide your arm down until your elbow is at your side. As your training partner is pinning your arms tightly, you will:

1. Move your feet as close to your buttocks as comfortably possible. Your knees will be together.
2. Slide one arm toward your head or slide the elbow into your side. The balance of your antagonist will start shifting. At the same time, you will buck your hips as hard as you can in the direction of wherever you slid your hands. This will accelerate his shift in balance, and you can easily roll over onto him, bringing your forearm to his trachea and your knee to his groin as you go. As before, practice slowly and without stress from your training partner. You can induce stress as your skills progress.

DANGER AT THE CAR

The car is where many assaults on women take place. The principles remain the same when grabbed or picked up from behind. Strike the groin to achieve an injury and buy time for the subsequent injuries.

Figure 55. Assaults against women often take place when they are distracted while loading a car.

Figure 56. "Groin, groin, groin!"

Figure 57. After attacking the groin, find the next target. In this case, she will use the ulna bone of her arm against his throat. She will engage her body weight into the strike by stepping through her antagonist. Back foot flat and back leg straight.

Figure 58. Injured people move away from the injury, thereby setting her up for the next target.

Figure 59. A kick to the groin with the shin or the ball of the foot.

Figure 60. With your antagonist bent over from the kick to the groin, his neck provides the perfect target. Step into the strike with a flat foot and straight back leg to engage your body weight into the strike.

If you don't live in San Diego, I would highly recommend going at least once to an Injury Dynamics training weekend (you can see when training is available by visiting InjuryDynamics. com) in order to get the basic techniques in person. And between a trip to SeaWorld and Disneyland in Los Angeles, make it a point to also visit Scott Babb of Libre if you want to learn the basics of offensive knife fighting. But what if you simply cannot? Fear not, the beauty of the internet is such that you can join Target Focused Training, Injury Dynamics, and Libre online. Then your task will be to find at least one training partner—and there are hundreds, if not thousands, of them scattered across the country—or work with a friend. The advent of the internet has had a tremendous impact on the martial arts world (both good and bad). With the online training, however, you can watch a technique 10,000 times—it's an excellent 90 percent solution.

Krav Maga in general is a good, no-nonsense style if you can't get access to Injury Dynamics (it was a colleague of mine who is heavily into Krav who introduced me to TFT)—the point being that not all martial arts are created equally. It depends on the teacher and the system itself.

Remember that the most proficient killers in our society (mostly inhabiting our nation's jail systems) understand they need surprise and overwhelming violence to get what they want. They have the intent to get it done and they know what works. And there is a lot to be learned from that. We can't all be sheepdogs, but we can learn to fight like a wolf to defeat a wolf. And we don't need to be encumbered by degrees of restraint like the sheepdogs. Learn how to turn on violence like a sociopath when you need it but then rejoin the flock as a peace-loving sheep afterward because, after all, it's the sheep who make the world beautiful.

Susan Kuhnhausen was no stranger to violence as an emergency room nurse, and while she won her incredible fourteen-minute life-and-death marathon struggle against her claw hammer wielding, fifty-nine-year-old assailant, just imagine how she might have fared with a bit of Injury Dynamics training under her belt. (Fortunately, biting testicles is not in Chris's repertoire, but hey, if that's what it takes to get the job done...) And it doesn't take a lifetime of training, as do so many martial arts styles; rather, it takes some forethought and a weekend of training to start to ingrain the methodology and thought process to breaking another human being when your life is on the line. Learning how to use your body to break another person's body is akin to learning how to swim. You can learn just enough to keep afloat and stave off drowning, or you could put in the effort and time to master the butterfly stroke. While the choice that requires more effort will allow you to master a variety of water conditions, at the end of the day, they will both keep you afloat. Just a couple of days of training can be all it takes to make the difference between staying above dirt or finding a place six feet under.

After teaching a female colleague the basics of Injury Dynamics, she said she wanted her adult daughter to learn. When I explained that Chris offered weekend seminars in San Diego on a fairly regular basis and gave the approximate cost for two days' worth of instruction, she exclaimed, "That's how much we just spent getting our dog trained, and it didn't even work! Absolutely, I will send my daughter there!"

I love dogs, but for the cost of training one (and certainly less than the cost of buying a purebred—just ask the breeder who sold me my beautiful German shepherd—you can learn to effectively destroy an antagonist during the worst fifteen seconds of the worst day of your life. Go to San Diego and train with Chris and Matt—if even for a weekend. It will change your life.

FOR THE LESS THAN AGILE THROUGH AGE OR PHYSICAL MISFORTUNE: DON'T UNDERESTIMATE YOUR ABILITIES OR YOUR CANE!

I've taught people from their twenties to their seventies. People of any gender, age, and with physical limitations brought on by accident, nature, or the ravages of time and war can benefit from Injury Dynamics training. They only have to tailor it to their abilities, visualize, and train to the extent possible to imprint courses of action and proper targeting. The three targets on the human body that don't need complete body weight to destroy or injure are the eyes, throat, and groin. Raking the eyes with a free hand or a slap to the groin followed by aggressive attacks with the cane to those same targets can completely change the dynamic to your favor. A cane can be used to strike the throat in a two-handed grip, hands about a foot apart with the cane parallel to the ground. Similarly, a one-handed grip or two-handed grip on the cane to strike the side or back of the neck can also be very effective. But once this course of action is embarked upon, you must see it through—to the point where the antagonist is unconscious or dead. Age or disability does not mean you should submit to the urban food chain, but like any other worthy endeavor, it requires commitment, forethought, and practice.

Unfortunately, a certain percentage of people who learn protective measures or something like Injury Dynamics do so *after* they have suffered a traumatic incident. They are often driven by the fear they encountered, the feelings of helplessness, and postincident stress. Better late than never, but the amount of suffering to get to the point of learning can't be measured. Then there are the students who have successfully used Injury Dynamics in real life-or-death situations. Chris keeps a running tab of these incidents as motivational reminders that the hard work on the mats has relevance in the rest of our lives. As in any worthy endeavor, there is a tremendous sense of accomplishment and empowerment for any person who has successfully employed what they have been taught. Some of the people mentioned in the success stories (and several were women) had never been in a conflict or fight their entire lives, but they prevailed when it mattered the most. Do yourself a favor. Don't wait until after you suffer a traumatic event. Every journey begins with the first step. Take control of your options and begin now.

KEY CONCEPTS

- All martial arts are not created equally. Most offer health benefits (except maybe the no-touch knockout variety, which, in my humble opinion, is setting up the practitioner for extreme disappointment).
- Among the best for learning how to execute a violent attack under extremis are Injury Dynamics and Target Focus Training. Krav Maga is also a good alternative in terms of general styles.
- The advent of the internet means you can learn and practice in any location, although I would highly recommend a trip to Injury Dynamics at some point to get started, and then subscribe to their website to sustain and advance your skills. Find a training partner.
- Age and physical limitations aside, you still have options with self-protection. The same principles of slow practice and visualization apply.
- Learning to fight like a sociopath with your hands is like swimming: you can learn enough to stay afloat, or you could spend the hours necessary to win the 200-meter butterfly. Both will keep you from drowning. With a practical system like Injury Dynamics, you can spend a couple of

days to get the basics and enough knowledge and practical experience to save your life. Or if you choose, there is enough material to spend a lifetime refining and honing your skillset, just like any other worthy endeavor in life.

· Learning to fight like a sociopath does not make you a sociopath, but it just might save your life or that of a loved one.

13

MEDICAL EMERGENCIES, FIRST AID KITS, AND GO BAGS

THE VIOLENCE OF A CAR CRASH

In my six decades on this planet, I have come upon four serious car accidents and a motorcycle accident that happened moments before my arrival, and each involved death or serious injury for the participants. I've made emergency room visits for my father and most of my children at one point or another. Never mind two-plus years in Afghanistan. But by the time I reached Afghanistan, I had undertaken multiple first-aid courses, and the combined war zone experiences and training over the years ingrained in me the need to always be prepared for a medical emergency.

I have always wondered why every car in America is not equipped with a low-cost, functional medical kit. One would think that economy of scale would bring the price down. Unfortunately, the average "first-aid" kit on the market is set up for little more than a cut in the kitchen. But there are steps you can take to set up your own kit or purchase a military-style kit on the market. Interestingly, people are reluctant to spend money on such gear. They easily pay hundreds and thousands of dollars for cosmetic additions to their car but don't want to spend one hundred dollars on medical supplies that could save their own or someone else's life. Don't be that person.

Car crashes are extremely violent and horrific for the suddenness of the event. Bodies are crushed and wrecked, head wounds are prolific, and fractures common. And so it is in war—only with more traumatic amputations and gunshot wounds. But it stands to reason that a medical kit designed for war, if slightly modified, would have an appropriate role in vehicle accidents and domestic life in general. The modifications could include a reduced emphasis on gunshot wounds and an increased emphasis on splints, controlling the bleeding, and bandages.

COMMERCIAL MEDICAL KITS AND IFAKS

If any good has come out of America's ongoing nineteen-plus years of warfare, it has been the proliferation of military-style Individual First Aid Kits (IFAK) on the market. You can now purchase a decent IFAK in the $70–$150 range. What should your kit or IFAK contain? This is based on personal preference and familiarity with the gear. For example, having a nasopharyngeal airway 28F tube with lube is a good idea if someone's face is crushed in a car accident, but if you have no idea what it is for or how to insert it, then you must hope someone else at the scene knows what to do with it (you push it down someone's nostril to keep their airway open). And in this vein, I would recommend that you take all of the training you can get your hands on, as well as self-study, as there is a wealth of knowledge on emergency first aid available to the general public through the advent of the internet.

In the realm of preparing for the unexpected, then, having a basic understanding about stopping the bleeding and keeping the airway open could be absolutely vital in keeping yourself or a family member alive long enough to reach medical care. Given that about 40,000 Americans die every year in car accidents and many more are injured, basic first aid should be a skill that we all cultivate and prepare for.

So what might a kit contain? There is no dogma here, but you will want to be able to stem a serious bleed and deal with airway blockage. It will depend on your level of first-aid knowledge and your environment. The kit I keep in my car has the following:

- Three tourniquets to stop bleeding in the arms and legs
- Four Ace bandages (these are great for wrapping up any kind of wound or using as a sling)
- Rubber gloves
- Nasal airway tube
- Medical scissors (to cut through clothing)
- Two quick-clot bandages (to stem bleeding for gunshot wounds)
- Two pens and a waterproof notebook
- Chest wound seal kit with an air-release pen
- A couple of emergency energy snacks
- Pliable splint for a broken bone

Ace bandages are great, and the more, the better. They can be used for all manner of wounds and for securing splints. The kit would also benefit from a flexible splint and a bandana, which can be used as a sling or as protection from the sun.

As with everything else involved in preparation, you don't want to be coming into consciousness after an accident hoping that someone will help or the ambulance will arrive, especially if the injury involves a family member. Be prepared for the worst (and hope for the best). If you get nothing else, get a handful of Ace bandages and a couple of tourniquets. The tourniquet in particular is an extremely useful tool to stop a bleed. It is absolutely essential if someone is bleeding heavily, as with an arterial bleed. A person could bleed out in three to four minutes. You will never regret having them, but you sure as hell might regret it if you ever need them and don't have them.

GO BAGS—FOR WHEN IT'S TIME TO GET THE HELL OUT OF DODGE (OR THE WEATHER GETS REALLY BAD)

The first time I described the concept of the go bag to my adult daughter, she exclaimed, "Oh, that sounds like every woman's handbag!" Can't argue with that logic, especially having seen what my wife carries on a routine basis. But for the rest of us, what exactly is a go bag? It is an emergency bag that you can grab and go in an emergency, and the contents should enable you to survive for several days. Working overseas, I always kept one. Given the terrorist threat against American installations, one can never know when a bombing or ground assault might require an immediate need to get the hell out of Dodge. In a domestic context, one would be well advised to have something like this if you live in an area frequented by storm activity like tornado alley; the East Coast, where frequent hurricanes or snowstorms wreak havoc annually; or the West Coast, which has its share of earthquakes and forest fires.

The bag should be tailored to the environment and no bigger than a backpack. So, for example, in the Middle East, my go bag backpack will contain items that will offer protection from the oppressive heat, an extra medical kit, some money, contact numbers, and language cards. If I were in Afghanistan, my go bag would contain roughly the same contents but even more medical kit items, redundant communications and navigation gear like compasses and a backup GPS, and additional ammo. While in my home state of Virginia, I keep my go bag in the trunk of my car, and it's geared for surviving adverse weather conditions. I would rather have it and never use it than wish I had one in a survival situation. Once you tailor your bag to your environment, it requires minimum upkeep.

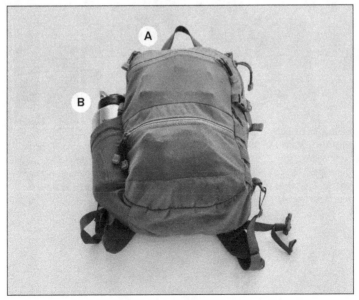

Figure 61. Sample go bag: (A) go bag with emergency items based on your situation; (B) water bottle and potential improvised weapon.

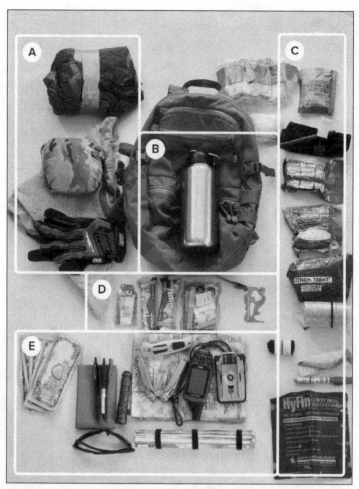

Figure 62. Major components of a go bag: (A) weather items, including poncho, wind breaker, gloves; (B) water; (C) medical items, including dressings for gunshots, Ace bandages, airway kit for nose and chest, and tourniquet; (D) energy snacks, fire starter, compass, and multitool; (E) money, flashlight, maps, GPS, improvised weapon, knife, writing supplies, and glasses.

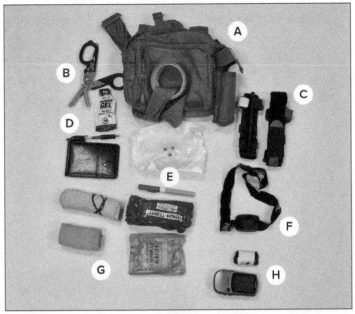

Figure 63. Simple first aid kit: (A) Medical bag with tape for securing bandages; (B) scissors; (C) tourniquets; (D) notepad and energy snack; (E) chest seal kit and ARS needle decompression; (F) headlamp; (G) Ace bandages and gunshot wound bandages; (H) rubber gloves and GPS.

KEY CONCEPTS

- Have a first aid kit or a commercial IFAK. Recent years have seen a marked improvement in emergency medical supplies. Every car and home should have one. You can purchase them fully kitted-out or put your own together. You should have a couple of tourniquets, a chest seal, something to stop heavy bleeding, and something for splints.
- Learn first aid. Without doubt, there will be a time where having a basic knowledge of first aid will come in handy in your family life. And it could mean the difference between life and death in a more serious incident, like a car accident.
- Go bags are more specialized to the environment you are in.

Once made, they require little upkeep and could become invaluable to your well-being in the case of an emergency. Consider your environment and modify as necessary. You will never regret having one, but you will definitely regret not having one if you ever need one and don't have it.

14

TRAVEL TIPS AND DOING AS THE ROMANS DO

YOU DON'T DRESS BY ACCIDENT (IN SPITE OF WHAT YOUR MOTHER THINKS)

Americans stick out like sore thumbs when traveling overseas. Backpacks, baseball caps, sunglasses, Hawaiian shirts, cowboy boots, tattoos, and logo-wear combine to scream, "Gringo!" Unfortunately, there are many parts of the world where simply being an American can invite a death sentence, at worst, or unwanted attention, at least. So the first rule of thumb is try to blend into the environment. Obviously, in some places, that is going to be very difficult (a Scandinavian walking around Beijing, for example). But dress down so that you don't look like an obvious target for terror; that is, someone sees you and decides to make an example of you for their cause. Similarly, if you are walking the streets of Jakarta, Manila, or Paris, don't dress in a manner that will make you a beacon for a mugging. My wife decries having to wear a full covering in Saudi Arabia.

Can't blame her a bit, but she has a choice. She can wear the covering and completely blend into society so that no one will know she is a foreigner, or she can try to make a political statement and not cover. (Frankly, I'm not interested in learning the consequences of that, but suffice it to say, it would not be worth the hassle.) In short, dress appropriately to avoid bringing unwanted attention to yourself.

LOCATION MATTERS—CYBER SECURITY

American businesspeople are targets all over the world. They are targeted either by competitive foreign business and/or by intelligence services. In some cases, those businesses work hand-in-hand with the intelligence services. This is an alien concept to American businesspeople because in our own system, there is a clear separation between industry and government. Don't believe me? Just look at Apple's refusal to help the FBI unlock the phone of one of the San Bernardino terrorists in December 2015 when they killed fourteen people and seriously injured twenty-two. But that is not the case in most of the rest of the world; where you go can have a huge impact. For example, don't take your notebook computer to Russia or China unless you don't mind revealing all of its contents to the security services. It's really that simple. Another unpleasant fact is that industrial espionage occurs even by countries we otherwise consider allies. So while industrial espionage and state-sponsored intelligence gathering is beyond the scope of this work, what you as the traveler abroad need to understand is that the more authoritarian the country, the more easily they can steal your data, and it doesn't matter if you are staying at a five-star hotel or an Airbnb. You can mitigate some of the threat by:

- Not taking your computer with you.

- If you do have a computer, keep away from public Wi-Fi hot spots (including hotel and airports) and assume that the host nation can access your accounts via those hotspots.
- If you must engage in electronic communications, use encryption and VPNs, but understand that if you are of high enough interest, the host services will be able to exploit your electronic devices.

The bottom line is that most countries in the world do not value or protect privacy the way we do in the United States, and most foreign telecommunication companies are either co-opted by the intelligence services or work closely with them. The good news is that if you don't work in the defense industry, tech industry, sensitive scientific community, or U.S. government, then the likelihood of you being a target is considerably less (except for certain authoritarian countries who might just want to check you out to make sure—did I mention Russia and China?). Rising tensions with Iran have seen an increase in cyberattacks against U.S. companies and government organizations. Belong to LinkedIn and work in the defense industry or government? There is a good chance Iran is targeting you with ATP34, a malware virus. As with anything else cyber, don't click on a link if you don't know the origin of the email. In one instance, the Iranian malware attack was disguised as a Cambridge University researcher. If you get a job offer or are contacted by an academic researcher out of the blue, delete, delete, delete.

ATTACKS AGAINST HOTELS AND PUBLIC PLACES

Since 9/11 there have been a proliferation of high-profile terrorist attacks all over the world. The vast majority were committed by Islamic militants with a couple of notable exceptions, one being the Las Vegas shooting of concertgoers in 2017. Taken together, however, it should be evident that these attacks can take place anywhere. Hotels, restaurants, business locations, airports, airplanes, and public events were targeted. Trucks have been used to run into crowds. Suicide bombings and stabbings were used to kill. A sampling includes:

- 2019 Nairobi, Kenya: Al-Shabab stormed the Dusit D2 Hotel. Twenty-one were killed and twenty-eight wounded.
- 2019 Colombo, Sri Lanka: Suicide bombers targeted three churches during Easter services and the Shangri-La, Kingsbury, and Cinnamon Grand hotels, killing at least 259 and wounding hundreds.
- 2017 Manchester, England: A radical Islamist detonated a suicide vest as people were leaving a concert by the American singer Ariana Grande. Twenty-three were killed and 139 injured.
- 2017 Las Vegas, Nevada: A lone gunman fired on concertgoers. He killed 58 people and wounded 422, and injuries from the ensuing panic caused an additional 400 injuries.

And of course, on September 11, 2001, al Qaeda operatives executed four coordinated attacks through the use of hijacked aircraft. Two struck the Twin Towers in New York City, one struck the Pentagon, and the fourth never arrived at its target, as passengers fought with the hijackers and the airplane crashed in Pennsylvania. The attacks killed 2,996 people and injured over 6,000 others. Thousands more suffered from respiratory diseases and cancers in the years following.

For many years after 9/11, the CIA had Americans from all walks of life joining the service as a direct result of the attacks. Now, however, our newest officers were children when this event took place, and as always, the American public has an extremely short-term memory, but for many of us, this became the single-most galvanizing event of our lifetimes.

What we should take away from these horrific attacks—virtually all against innocent civilians—is that we should remember that Westerners, in general, and Americans, in particular, continue to be prime targets of terrorism—not to mention criminal activity at home and abroad. This does not mean that you should not travel the world for business and pleasure, but it does suggest that you should employ some forethought and contingency planning, along with common sense and situational awareness, to lessen any danger you may encounter when you travel domestically or abroad.

STAYING AT HOTELS

We have seen numerous examples of four- and five-star hotels being targeted by terrorist groups over the past twenty years. Does this mean you should not patronize these places? Of course not—you should stay there. But wherever you choose to stay, there are a couple of things you can do to help mitigate any potential problems.

ROOM LOCATION

The people on the first floor are usually the first people to feel the brunt of an armed assault or bombing. So it stands to reason that the first floor may not be the best place to be. If you are on the second floor, you can still get out of a window. But if you are on the seventeenth floor, obviously that won't be a choice. Not to mention that most fire departments can't help you above the tenth floor, and in many countries, not even close to that. Know all the ways to get out—before a crisis.

HOTEL RESTAURANTS—AVOID STANDARD MEALTIMES

Hotel restaurants that cater to foreign tourists have been targeted over the past several years with increasing frequency. My suggestion is to avoid hotels that are known to cater to Westerners. In some cases, that might mean it's better to stay at a European- or Asian-owned hotel than at a U.S. chain. I would also suggest not eating during standard mealtimes. Hotel restaurants, when they are targeted, are targeted at the height of the meal hour. They are likely to be more crowded at noon and dinner than at other times during the day. And when they are crowded, they make more attractive targets.

THE OLD-FASHIONED DOORSTOP

Your hotel room is not secure. There are any number of people with keys to access it (the same with the hotel room safe). So when you sleep or are in the room, take an extra precaution and pack a hard rubber doorstop and position it on your door when you are in the room. It will prevent anyone from entering the room unexpectedly. And if you are asleep, it will create enough ruckus to wake you up so you are not taken by surprise. If you have a room that has a closet door that partially blocks the main door, then keep it open so that if anyone opens your door during the night (and gets past the doorstop) the main door will hit the closet door—again providing warning. Am I paranoid? Maybe. But do I sleep better in a hotel? Yup.

OUT OF THE ROOM—DO NOT DISTURB

When you leave your room, there is no sense in advertising it. For that reason, if you can live without a change of towels and sheets every day, better to place the "Do Not Disturb" sign on your door and keep the TV on in your room to give the appearance that you are in. Walk down any hotel hallway anywhere in the world and listen to the sound from the rooms. The rooms that are occupied transmit sound easily (keep *that* in mind during your next sensitive business discussion in a hotel room).

HOTEL SAFE FOR YOUR VALUABLES? NOPE.

Almost any hotel will offer a room safe, which I would opine is anything but safe (except maybe from your kids). In any hotel, multiple staff members can access your safe, and if a thief really wants it, he can in many cases simply take the safe and worry about breaking the lock later. You are better off hiding your valuables. Enter good old duct tape. You can place important documents or money in an envelope and tape them to the bottom of room furniture. Can a professional thief find it? Yes, but why make it easy? Thieves and intelligence personnel don't like to be searching a room a second longer than is absolutely necessary. Forego the safe.

PRYING EYES?

Recent advances in small camera technology means that almost anyone can put a concealed camera in a bed-and-breakfast or hotel room. Additionally, in every authoritarian country in the world, the host nation intelligence and police services have close (if not dictatorial) relationships with hotels. In other words, those services can do what they want to rooms when it comes to entry and technical surveillance inside of the rooms. Depending on the intel/police service involved, technical surveillance can be extremely sophisticated and nearly impossible to detect without the proper equipment. Or cheaper methods and equipment can be employed—it depends on how interesting you are to the service. In places like Russia or China, if you are a scientist working in high technology sectors or are related in any way to the defense industries, you are a target. But what about a host nation service with a smaller budget or the low-tech citizen who wants to violate your privacy with a hidden camera? One way to look for low-tech hidden cameras in your room is to use the camera function on your smartphone to look about the room for any infrared signal. While the naked eye cannot see the infrared signal, the camera can. You can test your phone's ability to detect infrared by hitting a button on the remote while looking at it through your camera function. If you can see the infrared signal light up in your smartphone camera, you can use the camera function of your smartphone to do a quick search of your room to look for any infrared cameras that might be hidden there. Far from perfect, but better than nothing when you check into that Airbnb.

DANGEROUS FUN

When a suicide bomber entered Paddy's Pub in Bali, Indonesia, in 2002, the plotters intended to kill as many Americans as possible. Their casing of the target sites revealed that they were gathering places for foreigners, and to them, any Westerner looked American. The bomber detonated himself inside the pub, and when survivors ran out into the street in the aftermath, a car bomb that was parked a short distance away in front of the Sari Club was detonated, killing in total

202 people—mostly Australians. The point is that some terrorist groups can't tell the difference between an American and an Albanian, and it doesn't really matter to them. The effect is basically the same in their eyes. And if a fellow Muslim is killed in the attack, they excuse that inconvenient fact with the twisted logic that God will provide an extra special spot in heaven for them. So when you are traveling and you go out for the evening, avoid areas and venues where Westerners are known to party.

DRIVING AROUND TOWN

Wherever I drive in the world, I have one habit that I employ no matter what country I am in. When I come to any kind of a stop, I always leave at least one car length between me and the car in front of me. A good number of abductions, smash and grab robberies, car jackings, and terrorist attacks against people in cars happen when the car is stopped, either due to traffic or because one of the attackers blocked your forward passage with one of their cars. But here is the deal. The average compact car weighs just under 3,000 pounds, and an SUV typically weighs about 4,000 pounds. That means you have a battering ram weighing several thousand pounds at your disposal. All you have to do is continue sitting while you literally floor the gas pedal and keep the pedal all the way down as you run over and through your attacker or crash through his car (or, on a good day, both). There are two points of possible failure in this course of action.

The first is psychological. Most people are understandably squeamish about the idea of running over another human being, even when they are under attack. Similarly, all of our driving lives, we have tried (some of us harder than others) to avoid hitting another car, and in the moment of truth, many people will hesitate. Don't be one of them. Mentally envision the act and how you would hit the person or ram the car. (By the way, using your car to hit closest to the wheel axle on your target car is the best course of action to move it after impact). A second potential point of failure is letting your foot off of the gas after impact. Again, this is instinctual based on trying to avoid crashing into someone all of our driving lives. So in sum, give yourself room and aim for the wheel axle of the target car to ram through it. (If you hit the soft part of the target vehicle, you run the risk of having your car get stuck in it). Finally, if you gave yourself room, you may have also given yourself the option to simply drive away quickly in the event of a carjacking or terrorist-type incident. There is one caveat here. In many parts of the Third World, any space you create between you and the car in front of you might quickly fill up with motorbikes like mosquitos in a poncho air pocket. If you are facing imminent death, chances are that many of those motorbike riders will also be cognizant and start to scatter at the onset of a violent incident. You may have to consider the consequences between waiting to die and potentially injuring some motorbike riders while executing your escape. If you think about it ahead of time, you are more apt to make a better decision than waiting for the moment of truth and then trying to figure it out.

DEFEATING A PICKPOCKET

Rome is reputed to have some of the best pickpockets anywhere. I recall hearing a story many years ago about a sign outside of a subway in Rome that warned: "Beware of Pickpockets!" What made the story so memorable was that pickpockets themselves put the sign up, and they would watch unsuspecting passengers as they read the sign and unconsciously touched the wallet in their pocket, thereby revealing exactly where the wallet was located. But pickpockets are active all around the world. If you are a man, carry your wallet in your front pocket; if you are a woman, wear your handbag to the front; and if you are in a city that has a lot of motorbikes, walk closer to the building than the street. In Southeast Asia, a common method of theft is to have two thieves on a motorbike ride up from behind a woman walking with her handbag and snatch it from her. Backpacks? Doesn't look as cool, but wear them in the front. Or better yet, leave them in the hotel.

IF YOU HAVE TO GET MUGGED...

In investing, even the novice knows that you don't put all of your money into one type of investment—you should divest. And so should it be when you travel. Don't walk around with all of your money. If, in spite of all of the advice in this book, you still become the victim of a mugging (let's face it, it happens), then consider having a throwaway money clip with a bunch of low denomination bills. The good news about a mugging is that if you are held up or threatened with a knife, chances are as long as you give up some money, you are good to go. After all, had they wanted to kill you, they would have done that from the get-go and searched your pockets as you lay bleeding on the sidewalk. So if you are held up and have a throwaway money clip, you can fling that down on the sidewalk, and then break land-speed records going the opposite direction. Clearly, you don't want to throw your actual wallet on the ground if you can avoid it because you don't want to give your home address from your license, credit cards, and other important items. Better to use the throwaway money clip.

Along the same vein, money belts and packets that hang around your neck and under your shirt are an excellent means for carrying the preponderance of your important documents and money. Take photos of everything in your wallet so that in the event it is lost, you know exactly what was in it.

REGISTER WITH THE U.S. STATE DEPARTMENT WHEN OVERSEAS

Either before you go or once you arrive, be sure to register with the U.S. State Department. You can do this online by looking up the U.S. embassy in the country and clicking on U.S. Citizen Services or elsewhere on the website. There is a program called the "Smart Traveler Enrollment Program" (STEP), and you can input your contact information. In this manner, the embassy will know you are in the country and can contact you in the event of an emergency (like accountability in an incident or information for an evacuation). You can also sign up on the embassy website to get SMS alerts for incidents. The American Citizen Services officers in the State Department are definitely the unsung heroes of the organization. Every time a U.S. citizen loses their passport, gets arrested, dies, gets scammed, mugged, injured—whatever, it is the responsibility of this section of the embassy to deal with it—which they do 24 hours a day, 365 days a year (and then some).

So to be clear, the embassy is part of the U.S. bureaucratic machine, and the Department of State, God love them, is one of the most bureaucratic organizations in government. The average citizen cannot just show up and expect to walk in to chat. But if you run into an issue like the aforementioned or an accident or are victimized, call American Citizen Services at the embassy. You will be glad you did.

Keep copies of your passport. It makes it easier to replace if you can accurately report what your passport number was.

KIDNAPPING THREATS—OR WORSE

In the late 1980s, Alfred Herrhausen was one of Germany's most powerful men. As the chairman of Deutsche Bank, he had tremendous influence throughout Europe in business and politics. For the Red Army Faction (RAF), a Germany-based terrorist organization that espoused a Marxist-Leninist-Maoist ideology, he was a prime target for assassination. Cognizant of the potential threat against him, Herrhausen had a security detail and an armored Mercedes Benz. On the morning of November 30, 1989, he departed his home at the usual time in his armored vehicle. His security detail was deployed in two cars: a lead car, and a follow car.

Shortly after departing his residence, the motorcade passed by a park. A bicycle with a package on the back was parked next to the road. About six feet past the bike, there was a small post with a photoelectric device. Directly across the street from it was an identical post with a reflective device. After the lead security vehicle passed the bike, a member of the RAF turned on a switch that activated an infrared beam that crossed the street. As Herrhausen's armored car broke the beam, the package on the back of the bike detonated and a plate charge was blown through the back door of the armored vehicle. The charge went exactly where Herrhausen habitually sat and took off his legs, which caused him to bleed to death. His driver was slightly injured and the security detail was unscathed. The RAF took credit for the murder, but who exactly participated in the assassination remains unknown to this day. The operation required careful, meticulous planning.

About six weeks prior to the assassination, RAF members prepared the wiring. Posing as construction workers, they cut a groove into the sidewalk for the detonating wire and covered it with material to blend into the sidewalk. The remaining wire was covered with some brush. The explosive was set to the height of his door and seat.

The sophistication of the attack—which was laser-focused on a single individual in a protective detail in an armored car—marked a new and dangerous development in terrorist activities, which suggested to many observers in the intelligence community that the RAF was likely supported by a state actor (likely the East German or Russian intelligence services). This type of attack was a precursor for what was to occur with alarming frequency in attacks against U.S. forces in Iraq almost twenty years later.

For a terrorist or criminal organization to plan your death or kidnapping, there are several basic actions they must take—none of which are particularly surprising. Let's start from the assumption that they have already identified you as a potential target due to your work title, citizenship, or position in society. First, they must locate you. This generally means that they identify your residence or hotel and your place of work. This takes effort and requires physical surveillance in order to establish your pattern of activity. Human beings are creatures of habit. We tend to leave for work at the same time, eat lunch at the same time, exercise at the same time, go home at the same time. We have favorite places, whether restaurants, parks, recreational locations, romantic haunts, children's schools, or sports activities. The more predicable we are in our movements, the easier we make it for those who would do us harm.

If we look at it from a tourism perspective, when we are on vacation or traveling for business, we tend to go to hotels and tourist venues that are fairly predictable. Certain nationalities (particularly from Asia) will almost always travel together with their own tour guides—replete with waving flags and bullhorns. Americans tend to be more independent than the average Chinese or Korean tourist, but we tend to favor more upscale hotels overseas. In the intelligence world, there is a belief (fairly substantiated) that certain organizations possess the skills to target you at almost any cost. The assassination of Alfred Herrhausen represents one end of the spectrum, but for the average citizen, we are more likely to be targeted while traveling to a foreign country for nothing more than being American.

In a domestic scenario, a criminal uses the exact same modus operandi—albeit with less sophistication and resources to study their targets. They are looking for the target who appears distracted, unobservant, and lacks confidence—an easy mark.

We've discussed general awareness in terms of earphones and cell phones and taking commonsense measures on the street, and the same rules apply to all travel overseas. The key to *not* making yourself a target (anywhere) is to remain unpredictable. This means reducing any patterns of activity you may find yourself engaged in, like going to the same venues at the same times, and varying your routine to the extent possible. It also means understanding that no matter how much you vary your routine, the two points you almost always have to go are your residence and your workplace. These are the two points of failure and where you should be the most vigilant. And while you can't change those two points of failure, you can control the times that you arrive and depart, and the routes you take to get there. The key point is that complacency does indeed kill.

KEY CONCEPTS

- Hotels and public places have been increasingly targeted by terrorist organizations. Avoid hotel restaurants/bars at peak hours. Know the alternate exits. Pick a room location that allows for an escape if needed. Understand that any number of people can gain entry to your room. The safes and Wi-Fi are not secure.
- Your electronic devices are vulnerable to exploitation, especially in places like Russia and China, but anywhere with an authoritarian government that can control telecom switches and hotel personnel.
- Have a throwaway wallet or money clip.
- Maintain situational awareness. Understand that those who would do you harm will have to establish your lifestyle. Avoid predictable patterns to the extent you can. Be the most alert in the areas around your home/hotel and workplace, as these are the points your watchers know you will always go to or return from.
- Remember that even people with physical limitations have options in self-protection. But it requires forethought, practice, and the will to see a course of action through to its conclusion.
- When you travel, register with the State Department's Smart Traveler Enrollment Program (STEP).
- Make copies of all of the contents of your wallet and important documents.

FINAL THOUGHTS— HOPE FOR THE BEST AND PLAN FOR THE WORST

The wheel of life has more than its fair share of trials and tribulations. These pages have covered some of the absolute worst in human behavior: sociopathic and psychopathic killers, asocial violence, gun violence, terrorism concerns, crime, and human conflict. It can feel overwhelming when considered in its entirety. The reality, however, is that humanity has always been this way, and in spite of the horrific realities of modern times, you are probably statistically safer now than at any time in our history. As a high school student in the late 1970s, I worked one summer with my brother-in-law's land surveying firm in Western Massachusetts. Much of our work was done in rural areas of the state, and I was amazed at how many old grave sites we saw in the course of our work. And especially how many of those old graves contained multiple family members or, in some cases, entire families whose tombstones were marked: "Killed by Indians." A reminder that more than 200 years ago, frontier life was extremely hard, as it was on most continents. Mob justice, war parties, no rule of law, slavery, hangings, feuds, and burnings were a part of everyday life in America and elsewhere. That we have come to where we are in society is a remarkable achievement in and of itself.

Many of our God-fearing, law-abiding fellow citizens will go through life and never have to contend with any of the ugliness described in this book. They are blessed or lucky (never discount luck) or both. Many, however, won't be as fortunate, and they will encounter various shades of gray in the realm of asocial violence, from robbery to assault to sexual assault to violence on the roadways to death. A very small minority will assuredly fall victim to seemingly random acts of violence, like the predations of an enraged man with a weapon or the calculated killing of innocents by a terrorist organization. Children, as throughout history, will continue to be victimized by adults and other children.

As the saying goes, there are no absolutes in this world except for death and taxes. What I would add to the death-and-taxes paradigm is this: if you take no precautions and trust your fate to the gods and luck that you or someone you love won't become the target of asocial violence, then I hope you win that lottery. But this is for sure: if you take no precautions and do become a victim, you will undoubtedly suffer greatly and possibly pay with your life. And you will never fully recover from the experience should you survive.

Conversely, you could take some simple precautions and vastly increase the odds that you will prevail in those fatal fifteen seconds. A major contributor to this success is increasing your level of awareness as you go about your daily life. Doing so will increase the probability of emerging from a traumatic event as a survivor, at worst, and a clear victor, at best. Either outcome is better than the alternative. The precautions outlined in this book constitute a conscious choice. It is the commitment to yourself and to your family, imbued in a good dose of common sense. Consider it a healthy lifestyle choice. Many people are happy to spend hours at the gym but might consider some of the measures in this book a step too far for their perceived circumstances. But circumstances change, and I would contend that just as exercise is a lifestyle choice, so too is adopting some of the precautions outlined here. Many of the precautions outlined require some forethought and effort in application; others, such as security systems, learning to fight, and weapons, require expenditures in money and time.

It is my profound hope that the group of people most victimized in societies throughout the world—women—can benefit from the amalgam of experience in these pages. As a husband to a wonderful wife and father of two daughters, I don't want them—or any of my children—to ever be in a position of helplessness. I want them to have choices and to be confident in their abilities. They will have to think about the unthinkable and work out step by step how they would tackle the challenge and fight for their very lives or those of their family should that event ever occur. All the precautions outlined in these pages are achievable. The one that will require a greater commitment is learning to use your body to break another human being. This, too, is within everyone's grasp irrespective of age or gender. Several of my students are in their seventies and can easily crush an opponent's throat, contuse an eye, or crush their opponent's testicle. Using 110 pounds of thrust to your opponent's throat is just as effective if those 110 pounds belong to a twenty-year-old woman or a seventy-three-year-old man. You can learn enough to get by or make it a lifetime study or something in between. That way if/when a nightmare scenario is ever thrust upon you, you will already have a way forward and a skillset in your list of experiences that you can draw upon.

The advent of the internet has revolutionized learning. It allows for having private lessons by once-in-a-generation experts, like Chris Ranck-Buhr through Injury Dynamics and Target Focus Training. Libre Knife Fighting also has an online presence. And for firearms, the NRA—gun politics aside—has a wide selection of quality courses online to enhance your skill and safety awareness with firearms. With many courses, you can view the instruction twenty-four hours a day at your leisure. This is a singularly phenomenal development in the world of practical combatives and unheard of a mere twenty years ago.

What an online course cannot do is imbue you with a mindset. They can inspire, but ultimately, that mindset must come from you. A decisive commitment to not rely on chance and luck to avoid the wolves among us but rather to actively seek out training and expand your horizons. A quest to work out, refine, and envision ideas long familiar but imperfectly absorbed. To think the unthinkable and determine in advance how you will defeat another human being who is actively engaged in trying to take your life. Chances are that scenario—if it ever comes to pass—will come after you are completely surprised or already injured. And that is the moment you should focus on the most in your training. All of the precautions outlined in this book will allow you to avoid trouble, or at least provide you with some warning so you can take a decisive course of action. And of course, always, always, plan for the worst and hope for the best.

But there are no guarantees in life. You could take every precaution outlined here and then some and still be victimized unexpectedly. But if you do implement some of the suggestions outlined here, and one day the universe singles you out through a confluence of events to test you for those fifteen seconds, at least you will stand a fighting chance.

ACKNOWLEDGMENTS AND READING LIST

REMEMBER YOUR TEACHERS AND EXPAND YOUR HORIZONS

First and foremost, I am eternally grateful to my wife, Dian. I thought I understood hardship, but when she was six and a half months pregnant with our youngest child, she was diagnosed with stage 4 cancer, non-Hodgkin's lymphoma. The way she handled the successive months of chemotherapy and the early inducement of our beautiful daughter's birth was simply amazing.

A couple of days after the diagnosis and exhausted from researching what it all meant on the internet, I remember she sat back and stated, "I'm really lucky. In the worst case, I have time to prepare my family. And in the best case, the treatment will work and I will beat cancer."

It was a profound statement, and she proceeded to live and breathe those words. She taught me what grace under pressure really meant. And she demonstrated it again when we had the three intruders outside the house while I was deployed to

Afghanistan. She is the kindest person I know, but she exhibited two distinct characteristics that were not necessarily apparent on the surface: do what it takes to protect yourself and your children and never give up.

The greatest hubris of all would be to claim knowledge on all aspects of self-protection. I owe all of the knowledge garnered in my journey and any successes I may have had in my career to the many mentors, instructors, and friends in industry and government that I encountered along the way. I have had the privilege to work with some extraordinary Americans at the CIA. Convention prohibits naming them, but as a group, the men and women of the Directorate of Operations and the paramilitary elements at the CIA constitute some of the most dedicated and hardworking public servants in government. At any given time of the day and at any given location on the globe, there is an elite segment of this population risking their lives for mission and country. Maligned in Hollywood and by domestic politicians looking for an expedient scapegoat, they carry on against formidable odds and equally merciless opponents at home and abroad. But they still get it done.

In the realm of martial arts, I owe a great deal to Chris Chan and Miguel Neri from U.S. Wing Chun for my early development. I am especially indebted to Chris Ranck-Buhr and Matt Suitor of Injury Dynamics, who profoundly altered my thinking on violence and how to deal with it. Chris Rank-Buhr, in particular, has a gift for teaching, and my only regret is that it took me over a half a century to discover him. I owe a special thanks as well to Tim Larkin, whom I've never met but whose Target Focus Training fired my interest in looking at violence and combatives differently than I had in the past. And a special thanks to Jay Thorne for introducing me to Sayoc Kali and teaching me how to cut "deep, wide, and frequent." Scott Babb of Libre Knife Fighting Guild for his guidance and instruction with the knife and Chris Robinson for introducing me to silat. Also, to training partners Jay Wakamatsu and Roddy Broome, whose professional and personal accomplishments are truly inspirational. Also to training partners Dave N. (another Krav practitioner), Phil N., Gardner P., Jeff T., Dave L., Rob H., Dave and Marcella, Tom V., Jeremy P., Phil W., and Irina B. They say you learn through teaching, and that is absolutely the case. Thank you.

Thank you to the kind folks at Scribe Media, particularly to Erica Hoffman for cajoling and pushing me when I needed it, and to Cindy Curtis, Zach Obront, Erin Tyler, Hal Clifford, Josh Raymer, Elizabeth Oliver, April Kelly, and Will Tyler for their individual efforts, guidance, and assistance.

A special thanks to David Rutherford, former Navy Seal and founder of Froglogic (teamfroglogic.com), who embodies what a teacher should be and prepared me for my first long deployment in a war zone.

Thank you to Anna Lind of Anna Lind Photography LLC for her support and to Krav Maga of Hampton Roads for use of the school.

I am greatly indebted to Sylvia Shaw, who literally toilet-trained me in the early stages of the wheel of life and, much later on the wheel, helped edit my jumble of random thoughts that constitute this book. And when that effort took her to the brink, she passed it on to Celest Martin, who agreed to take on the task of editing when I had reached a difficult crossroad, and her efforts took me across the finish line. A special thanks to Nancy, who recounted to me her terrible experience when she was brutally attacked within eyesight of her home—it is my profound hope that some of the precautions outlined in these pages can help someone in the future avoid the trauma of that kind of experience. To Daniel Montgomery, my father, who inspired me as an author, a citizen, and a man. He provided the moral compass in my life and inspired the love of travel, duty, and adventure that ultimately led to my choice of career. And finally, I am profoundly grateful to my children, whose love and curiosity for life inspire, confound, and enrich our lives immeasurably.

SUGGESTED READING

Among these key influencers in my journey, there have been several authors who have greatly impacted my outlook on protection, defense, and survival. Not just in an intellectual sense but in a very real way as I incorporated their advice, outlook, and philosophies into the execution of my duties throughout my career. These authors include people like as Gavin de Becker, Dave Grossman, Chris Ranck-Buhr, Loren Christensen, Tim Larkin, and Laurence Gonzales. Some of their works have resided on my bookshelf for years; others were more recent discoveries. All affected me profoundly. What follows is a partial list in random order of recommended books on subjects covered throughout the book.

The Gift of Fear by Gavin de Becker. How to listen to your instincts.

Protecting the Gift by Gavin de Becker. Safety for children.

Deadly Force Encounters: What Cops Need To Know To Men-

tally And Physically Prepare for and Survive a Gunfight by Loren Christensen. What to expect during and after violent encounters.

On Combat: The Psychology and Physiology of Deadly Conflict in War and in Peace by Lt. Col. Dave Grossman and Loren Christensen. The effects of stress and the value of mental preparation.

When Violence Is the Answer by Tim Larkin. Combatives.

Dangerous Instincts: How Gut Feelings Betray Us by Mary Ellen O'Toole and Alisa Bowman. When emotion eclipses common sense, by a former FBI profiler.

The Killer Across the Table: Unlocking the Secrets of Serial Killers and Predators with the FBI's Original Mindhunter by John E. Douglas and Mark Olshaker. A look into the minds of some of society's most prolific killers.

On Killing: The Psychological Cost of Learning to Kill in War and Society by Dave Grossman. Stress in combat.

The Talent Code: Greatness Isn't Born. It's Grown. Here's How. by Daniel Coyle. An in-depth look into slow/deep training.

What Every Body Is Saying by Joe Navarro. How to read body language, according to a former FBI agent.

Meditations on Violence by Rory Miller. Preparing for violent encounters.

How to Survive the Most Critical 5 Seconds of your Life by Tim

Larkin and Chris Ranck-Buhr. Combatives and the required mindset to win a violent encounter.

What You Don't Know Can Kill You by Marc MacYoung and Jenna Meek. Some of the legal pitfalls after a violent encounter.

Call Sign Chaos by Jim Mattis and Bing West. Leadership and preparation.

The Unthinkable: Who Survives when Disaster Strikes and Why by Amanda Ripley. How we react in violent situations.

Put 'Em Down, Take 'Em Out! Knife Fighting Techniques from Folsom Prison by Don Pentecost. Knife fighting from a former convict.

Machiavellian Knife Combatives by Scott Babb. Knife fighting.

Scientific Self-Defense by W. E. Fairbairn. Fighting techniques from World War II.

Deep Survival: Who Lives, Who Dies, and Why by Laurence Gonzales. An in-depth look at the characteristics of survival.

Thoughts on Violence by Chris Ranck-Buhr. Chris pens some excellent articles on violence and the human condition a couple of times each month, and they can be found in the members area of the Injury Dynamics website. They are thought-provoking and always an interesting read.

Finally, for additional instruction in self-protection, you can visit my website at GuardWellDefense.com.

ABOUT THE AUTHOR

ROBERT MONTGOMERY was an operations officer in the CIA for thirty-four years and served in some of the most dangerous locales on the planet. He's also a former Marine and the founder of Guard Well Defense, LLC. Robert teaches training courses, such as "Combatives for Women," "Improvised Weapons," and "Street Smarts for Students and Business Persons," designed to help anyone mitigate and deal with unexpected violence. He is the father of six wonderful children and husband to an amazing wife.

9 781544 509488